D0201862

THE
COMPLETE

the world of

Harry Potter

by Tere Stouffer

This book was not authorized, prepared, approved, licensed, or endorsed by J.K. Rowling, Scholastic,
Warner Bros., or any other individual or entity associated with the HARRY POTTER books or movies.

ALPHA

A m   c.

ALPHA BOOKS

Published by the Penguin Group

Penguin Group (USA) Inc., 375 Hudson Street, New York, New York 10014, USA

Penguin Group (Canada), 90 Eglinton Avenue East, Suite 700, Toronto, Ontario M4P 2Y3, Canada (a division of Pearson Penguin Canada Inc.)

Penguin Books Ltd., 80 Strand, London WC2R 0RL, England

Penguin Ireland, 25 St. Stephen's Green, Dublin 2, Ireland (a division of Penguin Books Ltd.)

Penguin Group (Australia), 250 Camberwell Road, Camberwell, Victoria 3124, Australia (a division of Pearson Australia Group Pty. Ltd.)

Penguin Books India Pvt. Ltd., 11 Community Centre, Panchsheel Park, New Delhi—110 017, India

Penguin Group (NZ), 67 Apollo Drive, Rosedale, North Shore, Auckland 1311, New Zealand (a division of Pearson New Zealand Ltd.)

Penguin Books (South Africa) (Pty.) Ltd., 24 Sturdee Avenue, Rosebank, Johannesburg 2196, South Africa

Penguin Books Ltd., Registered Offices: 80 Strand, London WC2R 0RL, England

International Standard Book Number: 978-1-59257-599-2
Library of Congress Catalog Card Number: 2007926846

09   08   07   8   7   6   5   4   3   2   1

Interpretation of the printing code: The rightmost number of the first series of numbers is the year of the book's printing; the rightmost number of the second series of numbers is the number of the book's printing. For example, a printing code of 07-1 shows that the first printing occurred in 2007.

Printed in the United States of America

Note: This publication contains the opinions and ideas of its author. It is intended to provide helpful and informative material on the subject matter covered. It is sold with the understanding that the author and publisher are not engaged in rendering professional services in the book. If the reader requires personal assistance or advice, a competent professional should be consulted.

The author and publisher specifically disclaim any responsibility for any liability, loss, or risk, personal or otherwise, which is incurred as a consequence, directly or indirectly, of the use and application of any of the contents of this book.

Most Alpha books are available at special quantity discounts for bulk purchases for sales promotions, premiums, fund-raising, or educational use. Special books, or book excerpts, can also be created to fit specific needs.

For details, write: Special Markets, Alpha Books, 375 Hudson Street, New York, NY 10014.

Publisher: *Marie Butler-Knight*
Editorial Director: *Mike Sanders*
Managing Editor: *Billy Fields*
Acquisitions Editor: *Michele Wells*
Development Editor: *Lynn Northrup*
Production Editor: *Megan Douglass*

Copy Editor: *Emily Garner*
Illustrator: *Carl Feryok*
Cover/Book Designer: *Kurt Owens*
Indexer: *Johnna Vanhoose Dinse*
Layout: *Brian Massey*
Proofreader: *Aaron Black*

To J.K. Rowling, for giving us a reason
to stand in line at midnight, time and time again.

Contents at a Glance

Contents

Introduction

The book you hold in your hands gives you an in-depth look at the world of Harry Potter in only 16 chapters. In these pages, you won't find character sketches, plot summaries, or details about who said what on which page of which novel. Instead, you get to explore J.K. Rowling's genius even more deeply, discovering the background of terminology, characters, places, and ideas throughout her novels.

Every detail created by Rowling has been researched to determine how she may have chosen that particular setting, that incantation for a spell, or that age-old symbol that has appeared in fantasy literature for centuries. Greek, Roman, and Celtic mythological similarities are explored. Latin, Greek, French, and Italian phrases are translated. Literary and Biblical characters are reintroduced, as are folk- and fairytale patterns. And comparisons to J.R.R. Tolkien's *The Lord of the Rings*, C.S. Lewis's *The Chronicles of Narnia*, Ursula Le Guin's *Earthsea*, and other fantasy classics are made.

Along the way, you'll recall details of the wizarding world that you may have forgotten, or, if you've never read the *Harry Potter* novels, you'll have a chance to read them with informed eyes.

How to Use This Book

This book can be read cover to cover, or it can be used as a resource, reading only the chapters or sections on which you want to learn more about the wizarding world. If you want to get a complete education, sit down at Chapter 1 and read straight through. By the end of the book, you'll not only have an excellent understanding of the origins and background of Rowling's work but also a greater appreciation of the genius of her creativity. Few of the hundreds of names, incantations, and places in her novels were selected without a reason.

To use this book as a quick, get-in-get-out resource, flip to the Table of Contents or Index and start with your most pressing questions. From there, read only the chapters and sections that appeal to you. You'll find that each chapter and section is self-contained and does not rely on your having read the section or chapters before.

This book is divided into five parts:

Part 1, "Wizards, Monsters, and Creatures of All Sorts," teaches you a little wizarding lingo, introduces the most famous wizards and witches, and gives you the scoop on creatures of all shapes and sizes.

Part 2, "Where and How the Wizards Are," gets you acquainted with the way wizards live their everyday lives, from how they dress to what they eat to how they travel around town.

Part 3, "Magical Places," takes you on a tour of the wizarding hot-spots in both London and Hogsmeade and gives you the lowdown on Hogwarts School and other wizard schools around the globe.

Part 4, "Spells, Potions, and Other Ways of Performing Magic," reveals the botanical, linguistic, literary, and mythological background on hundreds of herbs, potions, and spells. You also get the goods on advanced wizardry that's reserved for the talented few.

Part 5, "Regulating Magic and the Wizards Who Perform It," introduces you to Ministry of Magic officials, shares information about their departments, and lets you see how crimes are punished in the magical world. This part also offers a final chapter that gives you the lowdown on Rowling's seventh novel, *Harry Potter and the Deathly Hallows*, describing wizarding phenomena that don't exist in the other six novels.

Extras

Throughout this book you'll find three types of boxes that will make understanding the wizarding world even easier:

King's English

Can't make heads or tales of all those British terms sprinkled throughout the *Harry Potter* novels? This box contains quick translations of British terms and customs that may be unfamiliar to you, and defines wizard terminology as well.

Tourist Tip

One of the best ways to enjoy the wizarding world is to get out and see the sights around the world. This box tells you where you can travel (real or imagined) to bring you that much closer to where the wizards are.

Magic Tale

Want additional literary and mythological background for the wizarding world? This box brings you up to speed on how Rowling's work ties in with mythology, folklore, Biblical tales, and other fantasy literature. It also includes some related information to enhance your understanding of the text.

Acknowledgments

Thanks to Marilyn Allen, who took this idea to Alpha Books. To Michele Wells, who liked the idea enough to champion it, despite many unexpected roadblocks and interruptions. And to Lynn Northrup, Megan Douglass, and Emily Garner, who made the text 100 percent better and made the writing process as easy as possible for me.

Thanks also to illustrator Carl Feryok, the Legal Department at Penguin Group (USA) Inc, and the entire production department at Alpha Books.

Finally, my most special thanks to the following friends and colleagues, who supported the idea, celebrated with me when Penguin decided to publish this book, and offered a shoulder to lean on when the process got bogged down from time to time: Amanda Cockrell, Kimberly Dmytro, Dr. Janet Dunn, Renee Englot, Joseph Goetz, Natasha Graf, Loribeth Huck, Cathy Koon, Brian Kramer, Elizabeth Kuball, Marcia Larkin, Dave Milner, Dr. Julie Pfeiffer, Taylor Poling, Lara Saguisag, Laura Seybold, Brie Shannon, Paige York Sibold, Jenny Snodgrass, Anne and Richard Stouffer, Judy and Mike Stouffer, Dr. C.W. Sullivan, Sheila White, and Frank Wood.

Special Thanks to the Technical Reviewer

The Complete Idiot's Guide to the World of Harry Potter was reviewed by an expert who double-checked the accuracy of what you'll learn here, to help us ensure that this book gives you everything you need to know about the world of Harry Potter. Special thanks are extended to Nicole Notowitz.

Nicole Notowitz has been a Harry Potter fan since before the series gained popularity. She is originally from New York and currently resides in North Carolina, where she teaches second grade and shares her love of reading with her students.

Trademarks

All terms mentioned in this book that are known to be or are suspected of being trademarks or service marks have been appropriately capitalized. Alpha Books and Penguin Group (USA) Inc. cannot attest to the accuracy of this information. Use of a term in this book should not be regarded as affecting the validity of any trademark or service mark.

Part 1

Wizards, Monsters, and Creatures of All Sorts

Welcome to Wizarding 101. In this part, you acquaint yourself with basic wizarding terminology—words like *Muggle* and *Dark Wizard*. You also get to know some of the most famous wizards of all time, both from Rowling's novels and from rich folkloric history. And, best of all, you get to meet nearly 50 creatures and discover their mythological, historical, and literary histories.

Chapter 1

Wizards, Witches, and Warlocks

In This Chapter

+ Discovering basic magic terminology

+ Getting the lowdown on the most important characters of the wizarding world

+ Exploring the history of some famous wizards

+ Reviewing Rowling's biggest influences

Before we can wade knee-deep into the specifics of Harry Potter's magical world, we need a common vocabulary, both for wizarding terms and for a few key wizards. This chapter gives you both, detailing terminology you'll read throughout this book and giving you brief descriptions of the wizards mentioned most often in Rowling's novels, plus a few famous real-life wizards who have a place in literature and mythic tales.

What's What in the Wizarding World: Basic Terminology

Let's begin at the very beginning, with some basic definitions:

+ *Wizard:* This term has long been used throughout history, folk-lore, and written literature; it is synonymous with sorcerer, magi-cian, and conjurer. The word can be applied to both males and females in the wizarding world, but it tends to be used to refer to a male magician. Derived from the word *wise*, in the Muggle world it also applies to any wise person or someone who is excep-tionally skilled (as in, "he's a computer wizard!").

+ *Warlock:* Another name for a wizard; the two terms can be used interchangeably when discussing a male. (But not a female; a warlock is *always* male.) In the TV series *Bewitched*, males with magical power were always referred to as warlocks, not wizards. In the wizarding world, warlock is hardly ever used. The word is derived from the Middle English *warloghe*, meaning "traitor" or "liar"—apparently warlocks didn't have the best reputations!

+ *Witch:* A female wizard, also historically called a sorceress. (A male possessing magical abilities is never, ever called a witch.) The word derives from the same source as Wicca (see the following bullet). Witches have long been stereotyped as being ugly, ill-tempered old women, even if they have transformed themselves to be beau-tiful to the observer. Witches have also reportedly (in folktales) made deals with the devil to obtain their skills. Witches in the wizarding world are simply female versions of wizards, and they do not bear any resemblance to those two stereotypes, unless you count Dark Witches.

+ *Wicca:* A religion characterized by nature worship and the practice of witchcraft. The term originates from the Old English *wicce*, meaning sorcerer. Although Wicca is never mentioned in Harry Potter's magical world, those who attempt to ban the novels from schools often say they base their actions on the fear of their chil-dren turning to Wicca.

+ *Pureblood:* In the wizarding world, this term refers to a wizard born of two wizarding parents, who themselves were born of two wizarding parents, and so on. Only a few wizarding families are pureblood, meaning generation upon generation of wizards have never married a Muggle or anyone with a Muggle anywhere in the family. (At least, not that they admit to.) The term originates from *purebred*, which refers to a type of plant or animal (most commonly, a dog—for example, a Labrador retriever) that belongs to a single breed (also called a *bloodline*), generation after generation, without mixing with other breeds or with mixed breeds. Each breed shows specific characteristics; for example, Labradors are athletic, playful, loyal dogs who love to eat.

+ *Half-blood:* In the wizarding world, this is a wizard with one wizard parent and one Muggle parent, or anyone who has even one drop of nonmagical blood in his or her lineage. Most wizards are considered *half-blood*, a phrase commonly used to denote a relationship through a single parent—in other words, although you are fully related to your siblings, you are related to your cousins on your mom's side only through half-blood (that is, only through your mother). The term is antiquated today. A similar—and terribly pejorative—term is *half-breed*, which refers to children of parents of different ethnicities, especially when one parent is Native American and the other is of European descent.

+ *Squib:* A Squib is a child born into a wizarding family who just doesn't have *it*—no magical powers at all. By definition, a *squib* is a witty essay or lampoon, which is likely where the word originated: Squibs are considered a bit of a joke in the wizarding world.

+ *Muggle:* Someone without magical powers. The word's origin likely comes from the British slang *mug*, which means a victim or dupe. Several years ago, Nancy Stouffer (no relation to the author of this book!), author of *The Legend of Rah and the Muggles*, sued J.K. Rowling over the term Muggle. The case was eventually dismissed.

+ *Mudblood:* A pejorative term for a Muggle-born wizard (that is, with two Muggle parents); it comes from the equally pejorative *dirty blood,* which is the opposite of pureblood.

+ *Magic:* What wizards do; using potions or spells to manipulate a situation, control an outcome, and/or overcome the laws of nature. Often spelled *magick* in folktales and literature. The word originates from the Greek *magikos,* or "of the Magi"; the Magi were wise religious men, three of whom were said to have visited the baby Jesus upon his birth.

Magic Tale

According to Rowling, magic leaves "traces," which means that the potion or spell of a wizard will have the mark of that wizard. This means that if the rest of the wizarding world is paying attention, no one can get away with using a potion or casting a spell without others knowing from whom it originated.

+ *Potion:* In the Muggle world, a potion is a drink or medicine of some sort, although it tends to have magical overtones. Derived from the Latin *potio,* meaning "to drink," in the wizarding world, this is something a wizard mixes together, usually in a cauldron. The components of a potion include herbs, stones, and parts of creatures (eyes, tails, hearts, feathers, and so on). See Chapter 10 for information on herbs and Chapter 11 for more on potions.

+ *Spell:* In the wizarding world, spell, charm, jinx, hex, curse all mean virtually the same thing: something said by a wizard, with the help of a wand, that results in magic being done to an object, creature, or other person. Chapter 12 defines the most common spells and discusses the etymology of all of these wizarding terms.

+ *Dark Side:* Just like the Dark Side in the *Star Wars* movies, this is the bad side; the side you don't want to be on; and the side you don't want to run into when alone in an alley. Also called the Dark Force and the Dark Order. The term "sorcery" in literature and folklore has often implied the use of Dark Magic, although that is not the case in Harry Potter's wizarding world.

+ *Dark Wizards:* In the wizarding world, these are wizards who are on the Dark Side.

✛ *Dark Magic:* In the wizarding world, the type of magic practiced by Dark Wizards, including the Unforgivable Curses (see
Chapter 12). Dark Magic is deeper than simple magic that can
annoy or even defraud someone; instead, it has evil intentions
that start with a desire to frighten people, manipulate them, or
even control them, and eventually involves desires for absolute
power, world domination, and immortality. Dark Wizards, like
evil people in any world, possess a general distain for human life.
Dark Magic and black magic (a term not used in Rowling's novels)
are one and the same.

✛ *Death Eaters:* Dark Wizards who have committed their lives to
the cause of Lord Voldemort (see the following section). Because
they believe they can achieve immortality, these wizards are trying to "eat death."

✛ *The Order of the Phoenix:* Lest you believe that only Dark Wizards
are organized, a group of good wizards and Aurors (see Chapter
15) has twice convened to form The Order of the Phoenix. This
group's mission is to stop Death Eaters and Lord Voldemort from
gaining control of the wizarding world. See Chapter 2 for more
on the legendary phoenix and its presence in both the wizarding
world and Muggle folktales.

Who Who's in the Wizarding World

Although this book is not intended to offer plot summaries or character
sketches from the Harry Potter novels, you'll need to be familiar with
some key characters, and along the way, you'll discover a bit about their
backgrounds, name origins, and the like.

Albus Dumbledore

Albus Wulfric Percival Brian Dumbledore is a very famous wizard in
Harry Potter's magical world, eclipsed only by Harry himself and Lord
Voldemort. However, even if others are a tad more famous, Dumbledore
is recognized as the most powerful wizard of his time.

Professor Dumbledore is a deeply complex character; he delights in
candy, games, and jokes, but takes on the most evil wizard of all time.

As Headmaster of Hogwarts, he grows to love Harry, but he keeps valuable information from him, the lack of which causes Harry great pain.

Rowling is said to have used the last name Dumbledore because it is an Old English word meaning bumblebee, and she envisioned the aging headmaster buzzing and humming around Hogwarts Castle. His first names are interesting as well:

+ Albus is Latin for "white," which is the opposite of "black" or "dark." From the get-go, Dumbledore is identified as one of the good guys.

+ Wulfric was the name of a twelfth century saint who, upon meeting a homeless man in the street, gave up his career and fortune, took up the life of a hermit, and became a deeply holy man.

+ Percival was a knight of King Arthur's Round Table; son of King Pellinore and companion to Galahad on the quest for the Holy Grail. Some have suggested that this name also may allude to "pierce the veil" (veil meaning death), possibly alluding to an ability to return from the dead.

+ Plain-sounding Brian is a Celtic name meaning strong, fitting for the most powerful wizard of his age.

King's English

One of Dumbledore's titles is Supreme Mugwump, which is ironic, because "mugwump" is a decidedly North American, not British, term. To the Algonquian Native American, it meant "great chief," and that term likely applies to Dumbledore's resumé. But in 1884, the term was used derisively in the United States to denote Republicans who supported the Democratic presidential candidate. Throughout the rest of that century in American politics, the term came to describe a traitor or turncoat, a politician who waffled on an issue, and someone who's minor position of authority caused him to become obnoxiously self-important. Dumbledore fits none of the latter descriptions.

Tom Riddle/Lord Voldemort

Tom Riddle, although a handsome, exceptional wizard many years ago at Hogwarts, tended to frighten, rather than befriend, most people. As he got older, Riddle set out to create a world of pureblood wizards (which is interesting, given that he himself was not of pure blood … he is, indeed, a riddle!). As he gained power, Tom created the name Lord Voldemort for himself, a name that represents three French words: *vol* (theft), *de* (of), and *mort* (death)—"theft of death"—which is another way to say "immortal." In the second *Harry Potter* novel, Rowling also shows us that "I am Lord Voldemort" is an anagram of "Tom Marvolo Riddle," his full name.

In an attempt to gain immortality, Voldemort created horcruxes (see Chapter 13), in which he stored pieces of his soul. The idea was that even if his physical body were killed, he could still live. This is why, although he was nearly killed when his curse against Harry Potter bounced back at him, he was able to survive. Through the use of magic, he slowly regained human form, first by cohabitating the body of another person, and later by taking on his own human form, although he appears much more snakelike than human throughout this process. (See Chapter 16 for the final word on Lord Voldemort and what his intentions are.)

Because of his great power—and the fear his power instills—Lord Voldemort is often referred to as "You-Know-Who" and "He-Who-Must-Not-Be-Named." Even evil wizards who work for Voldemort abstain from using his name, calling him the Dark Lord.

Magic Tale

When Lord Voldemort inhabits another human being, that person has two faces, with Voldemort's looking out the back of the head. The Roman god Janus (for whom the month of January is named) had similar features—two faces, with one in the front of the head (the usual position), and one in back. In fact, it's from Janus that we get the term *two-faced*, meaning one who lies or tells contradictory information to two different people (that is, each "face" tells a different story).

Voldemort is, in essence, the leader of the Dark Wizards. Like Hitler's campaign to put Aryan Germans in charge and eradicate those of Jewish descent, Voldemort is a demagogue, appealing to the emotions of pureblood wizards, touting the idea of purifying the wizarding community by putting purebloods in charge and somehow getting rid of those born to Muggle parents. Pureblood wizards, who fear changes in their world, tap into that emotion and are persuaded to do evil.

Harry Potter

What better name for a common, ordinary boy than "Harry Potter"? A "potter's field" is, in fact, a cemetery in which people of unknown identity or the very poor are buried. Although a hero in the wizarding world, Harry is as common as dust in the Muggle world; Harry is overshadowed by his spoiled bully of a cousin, Dudley Dursley, who, like his parents, wants nothing more than to be ordinary.

Harry's story is a tantalizing one to young readers, who are at an age when it is normal to wish for and hope to be reunited with a powerful, wealthy blood relative living in a distant land. Centuries of folk and fairy tales tell the tale of a child ripped from the arms of a loving and powerful king or queen (or other respected person), "adopted" by ordinary people (used for slave labor is more like it—the orphan is usually treated badly), and eventually reunited with his or her true family (or loved by someone of similar rank). Cinderella, anyone? Harry's story contains many elements of this typical folk and fairy tale.

Harry, someone who is utterly invisible in his world, is, in another world, a hero, a sports star, and a savior. He simply needs to find his place, as do most children and middle-grade readers.

Magic Tale

Harry's story, although utterly unique in its details of the wizarding world, follows typical heroes' journeys in mythology and folklore, in which heroes are destined to save something (the country, the princess, civilization as we know it) and must overcome great odds (not the least of which is their own lack of skills, abilities, and confidence) to achieve that end. In the process, the heroes are themselves changed, from a boy into a man. They then return home a hero, as every Harry Potter reader hopes he will.

Hermione Granger

Every hero has a sidekick, and Harry has two of them: Hermione Granger and Ron Weasley (see the following section). Hermione is Muggle-born (her parents are, believe it or not, dentists), and she is an only child. That the name Hermione (her-MY-oh-nee) is from Shakespeare's *The Winter's Tale* (many believe Shakespeare's inspiration for the name was from Helen of Troy's daughter in Greek mythology; the name stems from the name of the Greek god Hermes) says more about her parents and their desire to impress people with their daughter's literary name than it does about Hermione as a character. Hermione, too, is extremely intelligent; Harry ranks her as one of the best wizards to ever study at Hogwarts.

The Weasleys

The Weasley family is a pureblood family that lives simply, in a house they call The Burrow. Unlike other pureblood families, they do not use their influence or magical abilities to manipulate others, enhance their wealth, or gain power. The Weasleys are all exceptional wizards and students; all have red hair, fair skin, and freckles; and all are loyal to Professor Dumbledore and against Lord Voldemort.

The word "weaselly" means to avoid commitment or responsibility, which doesn't fit the family per se, but that definition would match the opinion of many other pureblood families, who find the Weasleys' friendships with both Muggle-borns and half-blood wizards to be a betrayal.

Rubeus Hagrid

Part wizard and part giant, Rubeus Hagrid is a large, yet gentle man, standing head and shoulders above his peers, but often seen knitting or tending to orphaned magical creatures. He is Keeper of Keys and Grounds at Hogwarts, has taught Care of Magical Creatures, and was the first person at Hogwarts with whom Harry had contact. They remain good friends.

Rubeus is Latin for something produced from a bramble or thicket, which fits Rowling's description of Hagrid as "wild." Hagrid may come from the term "haggard" (or "hagard"), which also means wild, untamed, and unruly.

Cedric Diggory

The only student to have died in Rowling's novels, Cedric Diggory is portrayed as an exceptional student, wizard, and person. He died because he arrived unexpectedly during one of Lord Voldemort's plots to get to Harry Potter.

Pronounced SED-rick, Cedric is a common Welsh name that appears in both Sir Walter Scott's *Ivanhoe* and Frances Hodgson Burnett's *Little Lord Fauntleroy* (although Cedric was a bit of a sissy in the latter novel).

But the last name has an interesting heritage: the professor in *The Lion, the Witch and the Wardrobe* is Digory Kirke. When Digory was a young boy, he traveled with his friend Polly to Narnia, where he picked an apple that he brought back to save his dying mother. The seeds from that apple grew a tree from which the wardrobe was made.

The Noble and Most Ancient House of Black

It was likely not without intention that Rowling used the name "Black" for this wizard family, obsessed with their pure blood and turning to the Dark Side to protect the wizarding world from the effects of Muggles intermarrying wizards. "Black" and "Dark" go hand in hand. Here are the key players in the Black family:

+ *Sirius Black:* Best friends with James Potter while at Hogwarts and godfather to Harry, Sirius had a rather tragic life. Sirius is the name of a prominent star, the Dog Star, which is fitting, given that Sirius has the ability to shapeshift into a black dog. Sirius is the brightest star in our sky.

+ *Regulus Black:* Sirius's younger brother, who turned to the Dark Side and was killed by Voldemort, possibly while trying to do something heroic. Like his brother, Regulus's name is also that of a star—the Lion Star or Lion's Heart, the twenty-first brightest star in the sky. The star Regulus is known as the guardian (regulator) of the skies.

+ *Narcissa Black Malfoy:* Sirius's cousin; sister to Bellatrix and Andromeda; married to Lucius Malfoy. She is not so much evil as afraid. Her name comes from the Greek mythological figure, Narcissus, who becomes obsessed with his own reflection; this is where we get the word *narcissist,* a person who is obsessed with him- or herself.

+ *Bellatrix Black Lestrange:* Sirius's cousin; sister to Narcissa and Andromeda; married to Rodolphus Lestrange. She is definitely evil. Bellatrix is Latin for female warrior—and warrior she is, having killed many people. Lestrange is *le* (French for "the") + strange (foreign, uncommon, or bizarre).

+ *Andromeda Black Tonks:* Sirius's cousin; sister to Narcissa and Bellatrix; married to a Muggle, Ted Tonks; mother of Nymphadora Tonks, an Auror (see Chapter 15 for more on Aurors). She is not evil in the least. Like Sirius and Regulus, Andromeda is an astronomical term: a constellation (or group of stars) between Cassiopeia and Pisces. It is named for a princess from Greek mythology.

The Malfoys

Like the Blacks, the Malfoys are a powerful wizarding family obsessed with their pureblood heritage. Malfoy is French for "bad faith" (*mal* is bad; *foy* is faith).

+ *Draco Malfoy:* Draco (DRAY-koh) was the name of a seventh century B.C.E. Athenian politician—the over-the-top harsh code of laws attributed to him is where we get the word *Draconian*. Because dragons were monsters with many characteristics of serpents, the word *dragon* is derived from that Latin word for snake or serpent (*draco*), and the Latin has now also come to take on the meaning of "dragon." But Draco's name is not, per se, derived from the word "dragon"; instead, Draco Malfoy comes from a long line of wizards who were trained in Slytherin house, the symbol of which is the snake.

  Note that Draco Malfoy is a *doppelganger* (a German term translated as double-goer) for Dudley Dursley, Harry's Muggle cousin. Both are children without siblings who are spoiled by their parents and who, in turn, routinely mistreat others. But one character (Draco) exists wholly in the wizarding world; the other (Dudley) exists wholly in the Muggle world. Thus when readers first meet Draco, they have already been set up for such a selfish, insensitive person through reading about Dudley.

+ *Lucius Malfoy:* Draco's father, Lucius (LOO-see-us), is one of the most evil of all wizards; he is one of Voldemort's most loyal servants. Lucius in not an uncommon name in Great Britain; it is derived from the Latin *lux*, meaning "light" or "shining." Lucius

Malfoy, slick, handsome, wealthy, and powerful, does indeed shine. Two early Roman Etruscan kings bore this first name, as did three popes and the famous Roman philosopher Seneca.

Severus Snape

Professor Severus Snape, who taught both Potions and Defense Against the Dark Arts at Hogwarts, is notable because he was a former Death Eater who joined The Order of the Phoenix and became a double (or possibly triple) agent. The word *severus* is Latin for grave, strict, austere, stern, severe, and forbidding, which fits Snape's character perfectly. In addition, Imperial Roman Emperor Severus was known to be a cruel and calculating leader. In an interview, Rowling said Snape's surname comes from a village in Suffolk County.

Famous Wizards Through the Ages

Although the preceding wizards are the inventions of J.K. Rowling, the wizards in this section either really did exist or were so entrenched in folktales and literature that we feel as though they existed. All of the following wizards are represented on the cards that are found within a package of Chocolate Frogs in Harry Potter's world.

Tourist Tip

Albus Dumbledore is said to have defeated a Dark Wizard named Grindelwald in 1945, but no further information is given about this wizard. But you don't have to be a wizard to know about Grindelwald, which is a picturesque skiing, hiking, and mountain-climbing resort in Switzerland. Visit www.grindelwald.com for details.

Agrippa

Heinrich Cornelius Agrippa von Nettesheim was a sixteenth-century German *alchemist*, physician, theologian, and legal scholar. He wrote a manifesto on the occult, *De occulta philosophia libri tres*. Like Sirius Black's transfigured form (see Chapter 13 for more on transfiguration), Agrippa was said to have taken the form of a black dog upon his death.

KING'S ENGLISH

An **alchemist** was a person who studied an early form of chemistry, which was really part philosophy, part magic, part environmentalism. The goals of alchemy were twofold: 1) to try to find the philosopher's stone, which would have the ability to turn inexpensive metals into gold, and 2) to find the elixir of life, which would lead to perpetual youth and immortality. Rowling combined the two goals into one product in her first novel: a philosopher's stone (or, in the Americanized version, a sorcerer's stone) that produced the elixir of life.

Circe

Greek daughter of the sun god (Helios) and mother of the sun goddess (Aega), Circe (pronounced SIR-cee) was a sorceress who could turn people into animals with a single flick of her wand. She lived on the island Aeaea, where Odysseus and his men landed during their journey, and Circe promptly turned the crew into pigs. Fortunately, Odysseus had taken an herb given to him by Hermes, so he alone retained his human form. When Circe saw that he had resisted her spell, she lifted the pig spell from the rest of the men. A bit later, the child Telegonus was born to Circe and Odysseus, and as the crew was about to set off to finish their journey, it was Circe who warned them of the sirens who would try to lure the men to their death on the rocky coast with their beautiful singing.

Cliodna

Cliodna (CLEEV-nah), the daughter of the last druid of Ireland (an order of holy priests), was the Celtic goddess of the sea, the afterlife, and beauty. She was also said to be a shapeshifter who sometimes turned into a bird.

Nicolas Flamel

Nicolas Flamel and his wife, Perenelle, figure prominently in Harry Potter's first novel. Incidentally, Nicolas is also mentioned in *The Da Vinci Code*. A noted fourteenth-century French alchemist, Flamel was first a bookseller and scribe who bought a unique manuscript from a man in need of cash. The book, which discussed alchemy, led to his subsequent interest in all things alchemical.

The story of Flamel has taken on mythological proportions, however; he is reputed to have both lived an exceedingly long life and died very wealthy (much wealthier than a bookseller would have been), leading to rumors that he succeeded in both alchemy goals: the philosopher's stone and the elixir of life.

In Harry Potter's world, Flamel was also an opera lover and good friend to Albus Dumbledore.

Hengist of Woodcroft

Hengist of Woodcroft is perhaps best known as the man who founded the County of Kent. He was a king just before King Arthur's time, which is his likely link to wizardry. Otherwise, he was just a regional king who helped other kings in their battles.

Merlin

Entire books have been written about Merlin, the wizard famous for his role in the King Arthur stories. In T.H. White's *The Once and Future King*, Merlin tutors Wart (young Arthur) and helps him fulfill his destiny as king. Many believe Merlin was the basis for J.R.R. Tolkien's Gandalf, both being wise and noble wizards. Note that this wizard's name is frequently spelled Merlyn.

Morgana

Nearly as famous as Merlin, Morgana, the famous witch, was also an important figure in the King Arthur stories. Wart encounters Morgana (also called Morgan le Fay) in a castle. He later learns that they are half-brother and sister: Arthur's father (Uther Pendragon) seduced Morgana's mother, Igraine. Although both Morgana and Merlin are powerful, Morgana is angry and bitter, and she often uses her powers for evil.

MAGIC TALE

One of the wizards on the Chocolate Frog cards is Alberic Grunion, who is said to have lived from 1803 to 1882 and was the inventor of the dung-bomb (the purpose of which you can probably make out for yourself: dung + bomb). However, no such person appears to have existed in history. Several priests and saints named Alberic have been documented, but none in the nineteenth century.

Paracelsus

Auroleus Phillipus Theophrastus Bombastus von Hohenheim, whose nickname was Paracelsus (pair-a-SELL-sus), was a noted fifteenth-century physician and alchemist. He was one of the few alchemists who sought the powers of chemicals not for riches or immortality but to improve the abilities of physicians to heal. He contributed much to the medical field, including the idea that wounds can heal on their own, if free from infection. He also named the element zinc. Hogwarts Castle has a bust of Paracelsus.

Ptolemy

Claudius Ptolemy (TOE-lehm-mee) was a second-century geographer and astronomer who first proposed the idea that the sun circles the earth. His ideas became known as the Ptolemaic system. He was wrong, of course, but his ideas prevailed for over 1,000 years and gave Copernicus and Galileo something to work with and, later, disprove.

Witch of Endor

The Witch of Endor is mentioned in the Old Testament (1 Samuel 28: 4–25) when she conjures up the spirit of Samuel at the request of King Saul. Samuel's ghost then predicted Saul's losing his kingdom.

Where Rowling Found Her Muse

All literature influences the novels, poems, and plays that come after it, and fantasy literature is no different. As mentioned throughout this book, Rowling was deeply influenced by fantasy greats C.S. Lewis and J.R.R. Tolkien, as well as by Greek, Roman, and Celtic mythology; British folk-lore; and nonfantasy literature, from Shakespeare to Jane Austen.

In addition, there's no denying that the *Harry Potter* series owes a great debt to British fantasy author Diana Wynne Jones, who started writing novels in the early 1970s (when J.K. Rowling was a young girl) and continues to publish today. Jones is considered one of the great fantasy authors of the twentieth century; as an undergrad, she even attended lectures at Oxford taught by Lewis and Tolkien (lucky girl!). Some fans fiercely believe Jones is a far more imaginative writer than Rowling, but on the flip side, the popularity of the *Harry Potter* novels has recently put many of Jones's earliest novels back into print after a long hiatus. Both authors create fantasy worlds that, because they are so painstakingly detailed, become utterly believable. Yet both also relish silliness and absurdity in their stories.

Regardless of who's the better writer, Jones invented magical fantasy worlds that likely made a deep impression on Rowling. In Jones's novels, wizards and witches practice magic through spells; wear robes and cloaks; attend schools that train wizards; work as seers and healers; invite guests into a Great Hall for meals; stretch the insides of their houses to accommodate more people; plant annoying (attacking) flowers; drink from goblets; and live in a world with dragons, griffons, flying horses, serpents, owls, and other magical creatures. You'll even find a Dark Lord in *Dark Lord of Derkholm* (HarperCollins, 1998). Do all those features sound familiar? If not, read on!

Chapter 2

Creatures of All Shapes and Sizes

In This Chapter

+ Looking at creatures who are mainstays of Celtic and Old English folklore

+ Defining the classic creatures with Mesopotamian, Egyptian, Greek, and Roman roots

+ Reviewing creatures from other mythologies and folktales around the world

+ Inspecting creatures that came straight from the mind of J.K. Rowling

Creatures abound in the wizarding world, and most of them are not the least bit friendly. In this chapter, you not only sort through which creatures to avoid in a dark alley, but also discover the mythological, Biblical, and literary traditions of these creatures. Although this chapter discusses nearly 50 creatures, it is not an exhaustive list. Other creatures are lurking in the wizarding world, but they are not substantial enough to warrant entire sections in this chapter.

Creatures with Celtic and Old English Roots

The *Harry Potter* novels are British in origin and J.K. Rowling is Scottish, so it isn't any wonder that the novels draw heavily on Celtic and Old English folklore. The creatures in this section were all thought—by Celtic and Old English peoples—to exist, but sightings were surely rare!

Augurey

The Augurey, also known as the Irish Phoenix, is a small, dark-colored bird that, like a banshee, has a cry that predicts the death of the hearer. As with the banshee, people have died from a heart attack upon hearing the cry, panicked as they were. The Latin *augur* means soothsayer or fortuneteller.

Banshee

The banshee, also called the Irish Death Messenger, originated as a spirit or ghost who appeared to members of five select Irish families, foretelling them of their death by singing (or, in some versions, scream-ing) a lament. Akin to fairies, elves, pixies, and mermaids, singing banshees are always women and are usually fair, tall, and waifish, with long white or golden hair. Screaming banshees, however (as opposed to those singing a lament), tend to be more haglike than fair, and instead of being a messenger who gives a welcome forewarning—thus offering the about-to-be-dead a little extra time to put his or her affairs in order—are a messenger of death whose presence sometimes actually frightens a per-son *to* death. *Banshee* comes from the Irish *bean sidhe*, meaning "woman of the fairy mound."

Wizards, especially Irish wizards, believe in banshees as much as the next person, and these predictors of death in the wizarding world are not pretty: they are thin, greenish, dark-haired women whose shriek is unbearable.

Magic Tale

Ghosts have a long literary history, beginning with Apuleius's *The Golden Ass*, Chaucer's *The Canterbury Tales*, and Shakespeare's *Hamlet*. Perhaps literature's most famous ghosts are Banquo, the ghost in Shakespeare's *Macbeth*, and the ghosts who torment Scrooge in Dickens' *A Christmas Carol*. Gothic novels, at their height, also furthered the cause of ghosts in literature and led to the popularity of the ghost story, which continues even today.

Boggart

Long a part of British folktales, the boggart is a vexing but admittedly lighthearted creature that annoys people in small ways—moving objects around, touching or poking people, making noises, and so on. A similar creature is the Scottish bogill (also spelled bogle), a creature reputed to enjoy driving people crazy in little, annoying ways.

In the wizarding world, a boggart is a shapeshifter that appears to be whatever the nearest observer fears most; it lives in small, dark spaces like dresser drawers and wardrobes. A boggart is not so much dangerous as frightening, like its folkloric counterparts. A boggart can be eradicated with the *Riddikulus!* incantation.

Elf

From the Old English *ælf*, elves have historically been portrayed as tiny, lithe creatures, and may be either fair or dark in their skin and hair coloring. Also called fairies, pixies, sprites, and brownies, these mischievous—sometimes, downright evil—creatures are known to steal healthy human babies and replace them with sickly elvin children (called changelings), a story depicted movingly in Maurice Sendak's *Outside Over There* (although, in that story, the baby is kidnapped by goblins, not elves).

J.R.R. Tolkien's elves in *The Lord of the Rings* were unique to literature, because for the first time in literary history, they were no longer tiny, devious, and impish but rather, tall, elegant, commanding guardians of the earth and woods. No longer kidnappers or players of practical jokes, Tolkien's elves are among the wisest and most noble of all creatures, as well as phenomenally long-lived. Michael Paolini, in *Eragon and Eldest*, continues Tolkien's literary interpretation of the elven people.

Elves in the wizarding world are nothing like any elves in literature—neither impish little pixies nor elegant woods-dwellers. Rowling's house-elves are, instead, a form of slave labor to aristocratic wizards, who use them as free housekeepers, servants, and cooks. Elves are not allowed to own clothing, so they wear sacks or pillowcases and little else; if an elf's master gives him or her an article of clothing, the elf is free to leave that service and find paying work elsewhere, but most elves consider such freedom shameful. Most elves are lifelong servants (bound to one master for life) who despise, rather than wish for, freedom from their conditions. They know no other life than serving a master.

Tourist Tip

Beware bad dreams in Germany! Germans call nightmares *akpdrücken*, which translates to "elf-pressure," based on the notion that elves sit on the chest of a sleeping person, feeding terrible dreams into his or her brain.

Wizard elves are quite similar to wizards, albeit with quite a different look: large ears; large bulging eyes; skinny arms and legs; and short bodies. They think and act like wizards and are full of magical powers that they can employ without the use of a wand. Still, because of their low status, they are not supposed to use their magic and are banned from owning or using wands.

Fairy

Fairies have historically been thought of as tiny, gauzy, magical, female creatures who often fly, like Tinkerbell in *Peter Pan*. Unlike sweet Tink, however, most folktale fairies are devious, even dangerous creatures, especially because of their desire to kidnap human children (see the "Elf" section).

Fairies are not only a part of Celtic folklore, but are also present in the tales of such diverse cultures as ancient Greece and some Native American tribes.

Fairy godmothers, which are popular in Disney movies, bear little resemblance to fairies, except that they could be described as fairly gauzy-looking, and they are, indeed, magical. They tend to be grand-motherly types: older; plump; wise; and kind. Fairy godmothers are an integral component of fairy tales, which originated in the seventeenth century.

The wizarding-world fairy continues the pre-Disney, nongrandmotherly, nonsweet folkloric tradition, so fairies in the wizard world are tiny, wing-bearing, woods-dwelling, and mean. Fairies are hatched from eggs and cannot speak, thus bearing absolutely no resemblance to Tinkerbell or fairy godmothers.

Grindylow

Grindylows have long been part of British folklore, utilized as a concept by parents to keep their children from getting too close to ponds and lakes while playing. Grindylows are said to use their long, green fingers to grab children who come close to the water's edge.

Similarly, in the wizarding world, Grindylows are small water demons who use their sharp horns and long, green fingers to attack whatever comes in the water with them. Grindylows live peacefully with merpeople but attack just about anything else they find in the water.

Goblin

Goblins (also called hobgoblins or orcs) have a long tradition in English folklore. Because of their almost universal association with money, goblins are discussed in further detail in Chapter 4, in the section on wizard banking.

Kelpie

A kelpie (or kelpy) is a legendary horse-shape Celtic water sprite that dwells in lakes and seas with the hopes of drowning unsuspecting travelers; the same description holds true in the wizarding world. See the "Sea Serpent" section later in this chapter for additional information.

Leprechaun

An Irish folkloric creature, a leprechaun is part fairy, part dwarf: a diminutive old cobbler, usually bearded, who can lead a person who closely follows him to his pot of gold. In the wizarding world, leprechaun gold vanishes in a few hours, making it worthless.

Magic Tale

In Eoin Colfer's *Artemis Fowl* fantasy novels, LEPrecon stands for "Lower Elements Police (LEP) reconnaissance," a fairy version of the FBI or CIA.

Pixie

Similar to elves and fairies, Celtic pixies are said to dance in the moonlight, sometimes on the roofs of houses. Wizarding pixies, on the other hand, are tiny—less than a foot high—are bright blue, and have shrill voices. As far as we know, they do no moonlit rooftop dancing, but they do love practical jokes, especially those that involve hurling people high into the air.

Red Cap

A Red Cap is so named in Scottish folklore because this creature, who looks like an old man, wears a bloody cap. He is incredibly fast and strong, but he can be overcome by a victim's religious zeal. In the wizarding world, Red Caps are creatures that look like goblins and hang out wherever they can sense bloodshed (dungeons, battlefields, and the like).

Sea Serpent

The Old Testament gives accounts of several battles between God and a sea serpent called Leviathan or Hahab. In the Biblical book of Ezekiel, a sea serpent makes its home in the Nile, where God catches and kills it. *Leviathan* is still the word used today to describe a sea monster.

The best-known sea serpent (also called a kelpie) is in Rowling's own country: Scotland's Loch Ness monster, who is sometimes affectionately called "Nessie." Since the late 1800s, tourists and residents alike have spotted a two- or three-humped creature with a long neck who appeared, turned over boats, and caused both interest and panic. Photographs and videorecordings offer proof of Nessie's existence, although most people still consider the sightings either outright hoaxes or cases of mistaken identity.

Werewolf

From the Old English *wer* (man) and *wulf* (wolf), werewolves have long existed in folklore: people who shapeshift into wolves at night (whether the moon was full or not), attack or even eat people, and turn back into human form by day. Usually, one has to be bitten by a werewolf (and survive) to become one, although some werewolves are born with the power. Legend has it that scars obtained in battle while in wolf form carry over into human form, which led, at some points in history, to the panicked execution of people who had unusual scars.

Historians who have begun to look carefully at supposed werewolf (and, for that matter, vampire) killings see striking similarities to modern serial killings; werewolf and vampire legends may have been created to explain what was otherwise inexplicable.

In many literary cases, as is true in the wizarding world, werewolves are reluctant participants, who feel they are cursed to possess their shape-shifting powers. Wizards who are bitten by a werewolf will spend the rest of their lives changing into wolf form at each full moon, although drinking Wolfsbane Potion (see Chapter 11) does keep part of the man-into-wolf change from occurring—the body still changes into that of a wolf, but the mind does not. Fenrir Greyback is considered the most dangerous werewolf in the wizarding world, because he specializes in biting children, hoping for an all-werewolf society.

MAGIC TALE

Norse mythology holds that Fenris (also called Fenrir) is a great wolf who can be controlled only by magic ropes bound by gods. The Norse also give us the word *berserker* (from which we get the English "berserk"), a brutal warrior who wears animal skins in battle and is the likely origin of the werewolf legend.

Wolves, although not necessarily werewolves, figure prominently in Tolkien's *The Hobbit* and *The Lord of the Rings* and in Lewis's *The Chronicles of Narnia*. Werewolves have also been routinely celebrated in Hollywood, including 1985's *Teen Wolf* (in which the werewolf character is played by Michael J. Fox), 1994's *Wolf* (starring Jack Nicholson in the werewolf role), and three werewolf movies in 1981: *The Howling; Wolfen;* and *An American Werewolf in London*.

Winged Horse

Wizards view winged horses as a transportation boon, as they can guide flying carriages and, for long trips, even be ridden bareback. As with Hippogriffs, winged horses must be concealed through regular applications of a Disillusionment Charm, which allows them to blend into their environment.

Many breeds of winged horses exist in the wizarding world, but two stand out:

+ *Thestral:* In the wizarding world, Thestrals are great black horses with leathery wings and only skeletal bodies, who feast on dead cows and can be seen only by people who have seen death. A Thestral is also a term from sixteenth-century British mythology for horses that were believed by some to be demonic and by others to be quite practical. One tale links the Thestral to the winged horse Pegasus, from Greek mythology, as a brother.

+ *Abraxan:* These golden giant palominos can, in groups of a dozen horses, pull a carriage the size of a house. The horses have enormous heads and large red eyes, and they drink only single-malt whiskey.

Creatures from Mesopotamian, Egyptian, Greek, and Roman Traditions

The creatures in this section have a classical pedigree: they all emanate from the mythologies of Mesopotamia, Egypt, ancient Greece, or ancient Rome. A few creatures simultaneously originated in other areas of the world as well, but they're listed in this section because their influence on classical mythology was significant.

Basilisk

According to legend (from which Rowling clearly drew inspiration), a basilisk is a frightening snakelike creature; the name comes from the Greek word *basilískos*, meaning "little king," because a white spot on this creature's head looked like a small crown. One breath or look from this mythical reptile (born, oddly enough, from a cock's egg) means instant death. A basilisk is very similar in description to a mythical cockatrice, which can be killed only by the sound of a crowing cock.

The wizarding world's Basilisk has a few variations from its Greek counterpart in that it is born from a chicken's egg, and that egg must be kept under a toad until it hatches. It, too, has a deadly look that leads to instant death and it, too, can be killed by a rooster's crow, although it will live for hundreds of years if it doesn't hear that sound. (Clearly, Basilisks are city dwellers.) The wizard version of a Basilisk also has poisonous fangs, which seem unnecessary, given that one look instantly kills an approaching enemy.

Centaur

Creatures dating back to Greek mythology, centaurs have the upper bodies of men and the lower bodies of horses, and were thought to be wild, harddrinking, and cruel.

Conversely, in the wizarding world, centaurs are wise fortunetellers who understand the art of divination much better than most humans do. They are, however, aggressive and fiercely protective of their freedom, a result of having watched humans domesticate horses and fearing the same will be in store for them. Like horses, they vary greatly in size, color, and markings.

MAGIC TALE

Chiron is perhaps the most well known centaur; a skilled physician and wise counselor to Greek mythological heroes— Achilles, Asclepius, and Heracles, among them. He was thought to be the son of Cronus, a god, and Philyra, a sea nymph.

Chimaera

From the Greek *chímaira*, meaning young female goat, in Greek mythology, a creature named Chimaera is part lion (her front parts), part goat (her middle), and part fire-breathing dragon (her hindquarters, plus her fire-breathing ability). Wizards do not dispute this mythological tradition.

Giant

In the wizarding world, a giant looks vaguely human, but is built in gigantic proportions (20- to 25-feet high) with a very small head, no neck, thick skin, ugly features, and little ability to think, communicate, or get along with others. Arguments amongst themselves, in fact, are quickly leading to their extinction. This may be positive, in a sense, because, if influenced by Dark Wizards, giants could pose an enormous threat to both wizards and Muggles. But because they are so taken with their own internal bickering, they cannot be ruled by others. Giants live far from humans, usually in mountainous areas (where they frequently cause avalanches), because they were banished to those places by wizards. Like chickens in a pen, however, they now live in quarters too close to be comfortable—when giants live farther apart, they argue (and, therefore, kill each other) far less frequently.

Mythologically, giants are considered enormous, savage brutes, born of Gaea. In Greek tradition, giants were involved in a series of clashes (known as the Gigantomachy) with many gods, who eventually succeeded in ridding the world of giants. In more recent tradition, Gog and Magog were two giants who were captured by the founder of Britain. Literature's most famous giant, in *Jack and the Beanstalk*, fits the folkloric pattern of a dimwitted, brutish creature.

Although Biblical references to giants are rare, giants are represented much differently in the Bible than in the wizarding world and in mythology. In the Old Testament books of Genesis, Numbers, Deuteronomy, and Joshua, ancient giants are depicted as god-like men who were highly skilled warriors. That their size diminished their intelligence or reasoning skills is not part of these Biblical depictions.

Griffin

The griffin (or, more commonly, gryphon, from the Latin *grypus* and the Grek *gryps*) is hugely popular in mythology. Part eagle (upper body, wings, and head) and part lion (the rest of its body and tail), the griffin is revered and thought of as a protector of people, doing battle with one-eyed giants or men on Apollo's behalf. Although little else is known of the cultural importance of griffins, drawings and carvings of the creature abound in ancient caves and other dwelling places. In the wizarding world, griffins are sometimes used as guards.

Hippocampus

From the Greek *hippos* (meaning horse) and *kampos* (meaning sea monster), this ancient mythological creature has the body of a horse and the tail of a fish or dolphin and is mentioned only briefly in the wizarding world.

Hippogriff

A Hippogriff has the body, hind legs, and tail of a horse, but it has the head, wings, and front legs of a giant eagle, thus enabling it to fly. In the wizarding world, Hippogriffs are difficult to tame and ride, but if you approach them with respect, bowing and maintaining eye contact, the animal will bow back and allow you to come close, pet it, and even fasten a rope over its eagle neck to use as reins. They eat dead rats by the packful.

Hippogriffs originated in Greek mythology, but were first named by Ludovico Ariosto in *Orlando furioso*. Ariosto had long heard legends of a griffin—a mythological creature with the body, legs, and tail of a lion, and the head, wings, and claws of an eagle—being crossed with a horse. The word is Greek in origin (*hippos* means horse; *griff* is from the Greek *grypos*, or "hooked one"). A Hippogriff, therefore, takes the eagle portion of a griffon and crosses it with a horse.

Manticore

From the Greek *mantichoras,* which was derived from an Iranian word for man-eater (*martiya* + *xvar*), this demonic mythological creature has the head of a man, albeit with horns, the body of a lion, and the tail of a dragon. Ouch.

In the wizarding world, the manticore adds insult to injury by singing a little song as it eats its human prey.

Merpeople

From the French *mer,* meaning "the sea," Rowling uses the politically correct "merpeople" over the more common "mermaid" and the lesser-known "merman" (found in Tennyson's "The Merman"). Wizard merpeople are not especially attractive, as they are quite fish-like, with green hair, yellow eyes and teeth, and silvery-gray skin.

Mermaids, on the other hand, which date back to Mesopotamian legend, are fairies/elves of the sea, with magical powers that include, according to some legends, the sirenlike power to call men to their deaths underwater. (See also the "Veela" section for more on sirenlike creatures.)

Sirens were mythological sea nymphs—part bird, part woman—who sang seductive songs in order to lure sailors toward rocky areas, where the sailors would then crash and die. Hmmm. Sounds like a good excuse for some sub-par sailing!

Fairy tales abound of men who fell in love with mermaids, some of whom gave up their fish halves and became fully human; others who remained in the sea without their human loves.

> ### Tourist Tip
>
> London's Mermaid Tavern may be the most famous literary gathering place in the world, counting Sir Walter Raleigh, William Shakespeare, John Donne, Ben Jonson, John Fletcher, Francis Beaumont, Robert Herrick, and John Selden among its early-seventeenth-century patrons. Although it burned in the Great Fire of London in 1666, it once stood just east of St. Paul's Cathedral.

Owl

Owls and wizards have a long association. Because owls are nocturnal, they are associated with death, as was the case as far back as in ancient Aztec culture. Like the cry of an Augurey or banshee, an owl's hoot was said to foretell death among the Aztecs, as well as in Roman times. In Roman folklore, just seeing an owl in daylight was said to cause bad luck. Owls were also included in the lists of unclean birds in the Old Testament books of Leviticus and Deuteronomy.

Owls have also been messengers to and companions of mythological gods and goddesses, which is where they get their reputation for wisdom. Athena, the goddess of wisdom, had a companion owl, and this fact help elevate the status of owls from that point forward.

Wizarding owls function as messengers, although they are kept as pets and companions as well. See Chapter 4 for a brief look at how owls transport messages throughout the wizarding world.

Perhaps the most famous wizard owl is Merlin's Archimedes, who teaches young Arthur how to view the world from an owl's perspective in T.H. White's *The Once and Future King*. In C.S. Lewis's *The Silver Chair* (the fourth book in *The Chronicles of Narnia*), an owl, Glimfeather, hosts a parliament of owls to decide whether to allow the children to search for Prince Rilian. Finally, Patrice Kindl's powerful novel *Owl in Love* gives insight into the life of a girl who shapeshifts into an owl at night.

Phoenix

The phoenix is steeped in legend, which usually suggests that only one phoenix lives at a time, for an unusually long life. When its life is ending, the phoenix sets itself on fire and, from the ashes, a new phoenix emerges. Alterations of this legend have the same bird renewing itself again and again, as is the case in the wizarding world. Either way, the phoenix is a bird of immortality that has its place among Egyptian, Chinese, Christian, and Islamic traditions.

Wizarding phoenixes are, like the phoenix of legend, brilliantly beautiful, immortal, and powerfully magical. But they can also carry heavy loads, and their tears can cure even a deep wound—two characteristics that end up being helpful plot devices for Rowling.

Magic Tale

"Phoenix" is the name of two Greek mythological characters. One, the brother of Europa, goes to look for his sister when she is abducted by Zeus, until—get this!—he gets tired of looking for her and simply settles down to live out the rest of his life in a nearby city. Nice brother! The other Phoenix is a good friend to Achilles but suffers with blindness until Chiron, the centaur, cures him.

Salamander

Salamanders—small four-footed reptiles—are useful as ingredients in potions; otherwise, there is little magical about them, except that they look like tiny dragons. Well, that and salamanders in Greek mythology live in fire, but only until the fire dies out—then they die as well.

Sphinx

This mythological creature, widely considered a symbol of wisdom, is said to have the body of a lion and the head of a woman. In order to pass by her and enter the town of Thebes, she demands an answer to a riddle; legend has it the riddle was answered correctly only by Oedipus.

Magic Tale

Here's the sphinx's riddle: What is it that has one voice, and is four-footed in the morning, two-footed at midday, and three-footed in the evening? The answer: a man, who crawls as a baby, walks as a man, and uses a cane in old age.

Unicorn

From the Latin *unus* (one) and *cornu* (horn), this legendary animal may actually be based on sightings of a rhinoceros in about 400 B.C.E. However, unlike the rhino, the unicorn is a svelte creature, has the body and head of a horse, and may also have the tail of a lion and the hind legs of a stag. Always, however, a unicorn has a single, sharp, cone-shaped horn growing from its forehead.

The unicorn also has acquired a special place in the hearts of young girls, and it decorates pillows, notebooks, lunchboxes, and the like. This version of the unicorn is a silvery white horse with a horn. It's oh-so-pretty and is the horse of choice for budding princesses. Unicorns, in nearly every culture, are extraordinary creatures to behold.

Likewise, wizarding unicorns are highly prized for their beauty and magical power. Although some parts of the unicorn are used in special magical potions (chiefly the horn and tail), unicorn blood is *verboten:* drinking the silvery blood will curse you for the rest of your life, although it will save you from death even if you're seconds away. Wizard unicorns are fully grown at about seven years old; until that time, unicorn foals are gold in color.

Creatures from Other Folkloric and Mythological Traditions

The creatures in this section spring from a variety of other folkloric and mythological traditions, from Japan to Poland to the Middle East.

Boomslang

A boomslang (prounounced boo-um-slung in Africa; boom-slang everywhere else) is a large, fast-moving, highly poisonous African snake that's also called the tree snake. Boomslang is a relatively unknown snake that came to prominence in Agatha Christie's *Death in the Clouds* (1935), in which a passenger is killed on a plane trip with a dart poisoned with boomslang venom. The shredded skin is an ingredient in Polyjuice Potion (see Chapter 11).

Cat

Cats and magic have been linked for hundreds of years, in a variety of ways:

+ Cats and witches were nearly constant companions; cats were the pet of choice for single women (and, often, still are today), but a cat living with a single, older woman often led to a suspicion of witchcraft.

+ Cats were believed to have nine lives, allowing them to repeatedly escape death.

+ Cats were believed to be shapeshifters that attacked children in the night.

+ Cats were believed to be able to store disease; thus, a witch could transfer disease from a person to a cat, and vice-versa.

+ Cats were believed to have an effect on crops, either assuring a bounty or causing ruin.

+ Black cats were (and still are by some) believed to be bad luck, or even a representation of the Devil.

In the wizarding world, cats are not exceedingly dangerous or even interesting. They are simply common pets. Two pet cats, however, are worth noting in the wizarding world:

+ Mrs. Norris, the cat that belongs to the Hogwarts caretaker, was named for a character in Jane Austen's *Mansfield Park*, a character who was a snob of the highest order.

+ Crookshanks (*shanks* meaning "legs;" therefore, "crooked legs") is the pet of Hermione Granger. Bow-legged, highly intelligent, and a beautiful gingery-orange color, Crookshanks is part cat, part Kneazle, thereby accounting for its intelligence and discernment.

Note that, although dogs and wizards are hardly ever mentioned together, dogs do exist in the wizarding world. From a slobbering pet boarhound to a three-headed dog to the Grim (a black dog that predicts death), dogs have their place in the wizarding world.

Dragon

In both Western and Eastern tradition, the dragon is a gigantic, winged, fire-breathing, sharp-eyed, reptilian creature whose love of shiny objects leads it to plunder treasure, especially brilliant jewels and gold.

In German mythology, the dragon is known as the "firedrake," and in classic dragon form, it breathes fire, hordes treasure, and kidnaps fair maidens.

In Ancient China, in particular, but also to some extent in other cultures, the dragon is revered, not feared. In Asian traditions, however, dragons generally do not fly, and they also have the power to change size, even becoming so small as to disappear altogether.

In the Bible, dragons—often interchangeable with snakes—are linked to the Devil, an enemy of God (as noted in Psalms, Job, Isaiah, and Revelations), and this belief prevailed throughout the Middle East. Perhaps the most well-known dragon is in Chapter 14 of Daniel (a chapter that doesn't exist in many Bibles; when it does, it's often subtitled "Bel and the Dragon"), which tells the story of a dragon who is worshipped as a God. Daniel kills this dragon and feeds it to lions.

The wizarding world abounds with dragons, which are key to the banking industry, as they are particularly useful in protecting valuables. Dragons cannot be Stunned by a single wizard, so they are difficult to get past. Dragon blood is also full of magical qualities, as are other parts of dragons, which are used in potions. Dragon eggs are sometimes sold (illegally; the practice was outlawed in 1709) to wizards who want to try to raise dragons; the fire-breathing baby dragons are soon, however, too much to manage.

Several dragon species have been identified throughout the wizarding world, including the following:

+ *Chinese Fireball:* Also called Liondragon, this red dragon originated in the East and does (as its name suggests) produce a ball of fire from its snout.

+ *Common Welsh Green:* This native of the British Isles blends with the lush, green countryside and is happy living on sheep, not humans.

+ *Hebridean Black:* Another British dragon, the Hebridean Black is more dangerous than the Common Welsh Green.

+ *Hungarian Horntail:* This exceedingly dangerous dragon can breathe fire up to 50 feet in distance.

+ *Norwegian Ridgeback:* Like the Hebridean Black, the Norwegian Ridgeback has a line of sharp ridges down its spine.

+ *Swedish Short-Snout:* This blue-gray dragon, less aggressive than most, is the source of most dragon-related equipment (gloves, especially) that are needed to protect wizards from intense heat. Dragon skin (used in boots, gloves, and coats) is also just cool.

Four others—Antipodean Opaleye (with opal-like eyes), Peruvian Vipertooth (with exceedingly poisonous teeth), Romanian Longhorn (with, as you might expect, long horns), and Ukrainian Ironbelly (the largest and heaviest dragon in the world)—are known to exist in the wizarding world, but are not integral to any storylines.

Ghoul

Ghouls originate in Arabic folklore (called ghuls), where they are demonic shapeshifters who can always be identified by their cloven hooves. Ghouls even have cannibalistic tendencies. In more recent folktales, ghouls have retained both their abilities to change forms and their taste for humans as they change themselves into dogs or other animals, rob graves, and feast on dead bodies.

In the wizarding world, ghouls may live in wizard attics, but they're not cannibals—they eat spiders and moths and tend to be thought of as family pets. Otherwise, we know little about them and how they may differ from the ghouls of lore.

Gnome

In folkloric tradition, gnomes are old, often bearded creatures about the size of children but never youthful in their appearance. They are much like dwarves, and dwarves are, perhaps, the only mythical or folkloric creature not to have a place in the wizarding world—no dwarves are ever mentioned in Rowling's novels. (Dwarves, of course, have a rich literary status, from Snow White's seven dwarves to Tolkien's band of 12 dwarf travelers in *The Hobbit* and Gimli in *The Lord of the Rings.*)

Instead, the wizarding world is plagued by a common household pest known as the garden gnome. Not to be confused with the ceramic lawn gnomes that were popular in the 1970s in North America, garden gnomes dig around in gardens, wreaking havoc, and must be plucked out by a wizard, swung around until dizzy, and then heaved into a neighbor's yard. Garden gnomes, like house elves, score high on the list of Rowling's most unique and original interpretations of mythological, folkloric, and literary traditions.

Kappa

A Kappa is a water sprite from Japanese mythology, and like most sprites, it is a mischievous—even murderous—creature. Japanese Kappas in legends (and in some supposed "sightings") are thought to look like monkeys, but with scales and webbed hands and feet that allow them to inhabit small bodies of water. Kappas also are thought to have a depression atop their heads, which fills with water. However, if the water spills, the Kappa loses its strength, thus Japanese children were told to always bow to everyone they met, in case they met a Kappa, who would return the gesture and spill the water from its head. Oh, the stories we tell to get children to behave!

Fittingly, wizard Kappas are scaly, web-appendaged, monkeylike creatures who strangle anyone going into their body of water. As in Japanese culture, bowing to a Kappa tricks it into draining its strength.

Rat

Rats are the gerbils and hamsters of the wizarding world: rodents that are kept as pets. The fact that cats are also a common wizard pet does make for some awkward moments; a rat owner and a cat owner would probably not, for example, start dating. Rat pieces also sometimes make their way into potions (see Chapter 11).

Other wizard pets are what you might expect: rabbits; toads; snails; ravens; and owls. All have long associations with magic, witches, or wizards!

Re'em

Wizard Re'em are huge, golden oxen whose blood—like that of the unicorn—gives the drinker great strength. However, unlike unicorn blood, Re'em blood will not curse one who drinks it.

The Old Testament refers to the Hebrew *re'em*, which translates to "wild ox," although it has also been translated as "unicorn" and "rhinoceros." Either way, this is an animal with a large horn in the center of its forehead.

Troll

Sometimes synonymous with "giant," the troll originated in Scandinavian folklore as a creature who lives in a castle and terrorizes people. In later versions, trolls hang out in (or under) mountains and kidnap young maidens. Later, they camp out under bridges.

In the wizarding world, trolls are reported to live near Poland, and they are somewhat different from giants—shorter, for one, at just twelve feet high—although they do look rather similar. With exceedingly long arms that drag on the floor, wizarding trolls carry clubs that they swing around viciously.

Trolls—especially those that live under bridges—have been lurking in literature for ages. And take a close look at the trolls in both the *Harry Potter and the Sorcerer's Stone* movie and *The Lord of the Rings: The Fellowship of the Ring* movie. Same troll? Brothers? Cousins? It's eerie.

Vampire

A vampire, or revenant, is a legendary shapeshifter (usually taking the form of a bat) that lives off the blood of humans and, after biting, turns them into vampires as well. According to legend, a vampire can be killed only when a wooden stake is driven into its heart. Long given attention in Gothic tales, the most famous vampire is Bram Stoker's *Dracula*, which was turned into a movie in 1931. Anne Rice's more recent novels, along with the *Buffy the Vampire Slayer* movie and TV series, have kept both the legend of and interest in vampires alive.

Although not often mentioned in the wizarding world, vampires do hang out in pubs and associate freely with the wizarding community. They're not well liked, but they're not attacked with Holy Water, crosses, and stakes, either.

Veela

Wila (also spelled Wili, Willi, and Vila, but always pronounced VEEL-uh) are Slavic and Polish mythological nymphs or water fairies who are stunningly beautiful, with entrancing voices. Their greatest danger is that they seduce men with their beauty, such that men forget to eat, drink, and sleep. Although they appear human, they are not, and they can turn vicious in a moment.

Beautiful women who cause men to forget themselves, and then turn vicious. Hmmm. These tales smack of sour grapes on the part of men who have loved beautiful women and been rebuffed, but the presence of these fairies persists in legend and folklore.

Wizarding veelas are strikingly similar; they dance and sing as a means of entrancing men, but can turn hideous when provoked.

Yeti

The yeti, also known as the Abominable Snowman, is a twentieth-century legend of a Tibetan creature that appears to be part man, part beast and leaves large footprints in the snow. Yeti sightings were common in the 1950s, '60s, and '70s. The creature is described as being covered with white hair and standing twice as tall as most humans. Pictures of this creature nearly always show him running, and such pictures have graced many a tabloid cover.

Wizards believe that the yeti is actually a troll, or at least is a close relative to the common troll.

Wizard-Only Creatures

The creatures in this section spring from the creative genius of J.K. Rowling. Although similar creatures may exist in literature, these creatures do not exist in this form and with these names in any other writings or traditions. Where appropriate, however, the possible origins of the names are discussed.

Acromantula

Acromantulas are enormous spiders, nearly identical in description to Tolkien's Shelob the Great (in *The Two Towers*), a giant spider who drinks the blood of men and other creatures to keep her huge body fed. In the wizarding world, not just one but an entire population of such spiders exists in colonies, including in the Forbidden Forest. Their venom is valuable, but Acromantulas are difficult to kill and usually eat their dead, so the venom is nearly impossible to procure.

The origins of this word are debatable. The prefix *acro* (from the Greek *akros*, meaning point or top) means highest, thus alluding to the size of these spiders. *Mantula*, however, is not a known word, although many have postulated that it is derived from *tarantula*. However, just as likely, the name originated with a British sports car company, Marcos, which made, among other models, both the Mantula and the Spider. Both models were popular about the time Rowling was coming of age in Great Britain.

Bowtruckle

Bowtruckles are creatures who live in wizard wand-trees (see Chapter 3) and guard them fiercely, poking out the eyes of anyone who tries to take the wood from their trees without permission. They, therefore, protect the trees, a role of historical importance in Celtic mythology, when trees were considered sacred. Bowtruckles are the environmental activists of the wizarding world, the equivalent of someone building and living in a tree house for a few years to keep a development company from bulldozing a wooded or forested area.

Bow likely comes from the Old English *bur*, meaning dwelling place and from which the word *bough* is derived. (A *bower* is an enclosure made of boughs or vines.) *Truckle* is from the Middle English *trocle*, which has come to have a meaning of servility or submission. Hence, "servant of the boughs."

Dementor

Dementors are unique to the wizarding world: they are the prison guards at Azkaban who quite literally suck the happiness right out of people just by their mere presence. And their Kiss is even worse: most people, devoid of hope and peace, die soon after such a Kiss. See Chapter 15 for more on dementors and Azkaban prison.

Dementors are described very much like the Grim Reaper: a cloaked and hooded skeletal figure that seems to almost glide along. With such a description, they also call to mind Tolkien's ringwraiths, who are skeletal ghosts of men, too tormented to die, but still able to kill others and hunt down the One Ring that holds their power. The roles of the ringwraiths and dementors are quite different, however, as the ringwraiths live with the hope of returning to glory via the recapture of the Ring; dementors have no such goal and guard Azkaban because it gives them fresh resources (happiness, hope, and peace) to suck out and live on.

Diricawl

The Diricawl, although a minor wizarding creature, bears mention in this chapter because of its unique explanation of what Muggles call "extinction." The Diricawl is, in fact, the same creature as the dodo bird, which Muggles believe no longer exists, hunted as it was in its prime. What Muggles fail to realize is that the dodo/Diricawl is actually a magical bird that can disappear at will. It isn't extinct, but rather, hiding undercover for a while.

Doxy

Doxies (also called Biting Fairies) have fairylike little bodies and wings, with an extra pair of arms, but there's nothing cute about them: they're fuzzy, with thick, dark hair and they lash out with poisonous bites. They hide out in curtains and must be disposed of with Doxycide (see Chapter 11).

Inferius

From the Latin *inferi*, meaning "the dead," Inferi (the plural of Inferius) are corpses that Dark Wizards have placed under a spell and used as part of an army. These are not creatures who have been brought back to life or given the ability to think or choose, but instead are used as a shield and a means of frightening the bejesus out of wizards. Inferi are somewhat similar to the bodies in the Dead Marshes in Tolkien's *The Two Towers*, who look to be dead people with their eyes open, but humans who are alive are strangely drawn to them and can join them, if they're not careful.

Inferi is, along with Hades, the name given to the underworld in Roman mythology. The gods of the underworld were known as Inferi Dii.

Jobberknoll

The Jobberknoll is a small, unusual bird that is barely noticed throughout its life but, upon its death, regurgitates, in backward order, every sound it has ever heard, in a high-pitched scream. The name may be literal, in that a "jobber" is a middle man, and, in a sense, this bird acts as a middleman for all that it hears in its life, taking in all the sounds and letting them all out again later. (A "knoll" is a small hill.) On the other hand, the name may simply be a tribute to Lewis Carroll's Jabberwock, the monster of his poem "Jabberwocky."

Kneazle

The Kneazle is a magical creature much like a cat, but with the tail of a lion. Kneazles are fiercely independent and intelligent, with the bonus of having a natural radar for devious behavior in wizards. Because they can be dangerous, wizard owners must be licensed to own a Kneazle.

Lethifold

The Lethifold (or Living Shroud) is a deadly magical creature resembling a black cloak that floats along the ground. No, really—it's one of the scariest things ever invented! As if a wizard, vampire, or other such creature *wearing* a black cloak wouldn't be scary enough, a Lethifold is just the cloak, but it's deadly. It surrounds you, suffocates you, and then feasts on you. It's repelled by a Patronus Charm, but you have to be alert enough to use it before you're suffocated. Thankfully, this creature is rumored to exist only near the Equator.

The word Lethifold likely derives from lethal (meaning deadly) and fold (that thing you do when you put your clothes in a drawer). Lethe is also the river of forgetfulness that flowed through Hades—if you drink this water, you lose your memory.

Part 2

Where and How the Wizards Are

Everything you ever wanted to know about the everyday lives of wizards is in this part. Here, you get the lowdown on basic wizard tools: wands, robes, quills, and other magical gadgetry. You also find out how wizards spend their days—from cooking and gardening to sending mail, getting around town, and playing games and sports, including Quidditch, wizard chess, and Gobstones. And don't forget to read a bit about wizard and British cuisine!

Chapter 3

The Wizard's Wardrobe and Toolbox

In This Chapter

+ Locating the seat of a wizard's power: the wand

+ Looking smart in robes, cloaks, and hats

+ Writing the old-fashioned way: quills and parchment

+ Digging deeper into a variety of magical gadgets

A wizard's basic tools are simple: a wand; a robe (and, if it's chilly, a cloak); and perhaps a pointed hat. All are discussed in this chapter. In addition, various optional equipment is available to wizards: writing materials; Dark Detectors; and other cool gadgets. You get the lowdown here.

A Wizard's Most Important Tool: The Wand

A wizard without a wand simply isn't a wizard, because he'll have a tough time whipping up potions (discussed in Chapter 11) or conjuring spells, charms, hexes, or curses (all in Chapter 12). However, a wand acts only as a channeler of magic from the wizard; the lesser the wizard, the lesser the power of whatever comes from his or her wand. This is why, if provoked, a wandless wizard can make "funny" things happen (funny strange, not funny ha-ha). But for the most part, a wizard without a wand is a wizard without magical powers, because the wand focuses all a wizard's magical power into a small, but potent, space.

Magic Tale

Historically, nearly all wizards have employed a magical wand of some sort—whether a short rod or long staff—to cook up potions and weave spells. Circe (in Homer's *The Odyssey*) uses a wand to bewitch Odysseus's men; Gandalf and Saruman (in J.R.R. Tolkien's *The Lord of the Rings*) both carry staffs; the White Witch (in C.S. Lewis's *The Lion, the Witch and the Wardrobe*) carries a long golden wand; and Merlyn (in T.H. White's *The Once and Future King*) carries a wand made from *lignum vitae* (reportedly the hardest wood in the world; the name is Latin for "long life").

A wand or staff not only acts to channel a wizard's power, but also serves as a symbol of authority, drawing from its origins as a shepherd's staff. As a shepherd has authority over his flock, so do wizards carry authority over nonmagic folk. In the same way, gods and kings have power over their people, thus the ancient tradition of kings carrying a scepter (a highly ornamental rod or staff). Likewise, a caduceus (a staff with wings at the top and two snakes coiled around the rod; the caduceus is now the worldwide symbol of physicians) established the authority of Greek god Hermes/Roman god Mercury/Celtic god Lugus, who aided, acted as messenger for, and rescued many gods and goddesses. Ancient priests carried short rods; carrying on the tradition, Catholic bishops, cardinals, and the pope still carry scepters as a symbol of their wisdom and authority. Leaders of musical groups, whether a conductor or a drum major, carry batons, which can be small rods (as in the case of a conductor) or a large staff (as with a drum major).

One wizard can use another's wand in a pinch (or, for that matter, any nonhuman creature can "borrow" a wizard's wand, although that is expressly forbidden by the Ministry), but that wand will not perform as well as the wizard's own. Ultimately, there is one wand that's exactly right for each wizard. As the story goes, the wand chooses the wizard, not the other way around.

Wood Species and Sizes

Wands range in size from 7 inches to 16 inches, but could, technically, be any length. Wands are crafted from any of the following species, and based on the propensities of that species, may range from rigid to downright springy:

+ *Ash:* Ash is from the genus *Fraxinus* and is a member of the olive family. The wood is hard and springy, which is why it's also used to make broomsticks (see Chapter 5). Greek mythological nymphs (young, beautiful nature goddesses) of the ash trees, called meliae, were born when the god Uranus was castrated by his son, and the blood spilled onto the ground. In Norse mythology, an ash tree called Yggdrasil is considered the axis of the universe, not only providing protection and nourishment for all the creatures in the world but also bearing the wounds of the damage done by its inhabitants. Life literally could not have existed without this great ash tree. Also according to Norse mythology, the first man and woman were formed from trees, and the man, named Ask, came from an ash tree.

+ *Beech (or beechwood):* Beech trees, tall and gray-barked, tend to grow near lakes and oceans, because of their propensity for sandy soil. From the genus *Fagus*, this hardwood is light yellow in color. Beech is relatively inexpensive, and woodworkers find it easy to work with; thus, it's an economical choice for wand-making.

+ *Cherry:* This is, of course, the tree from which cherry fruit comes; cherry wood is a golden hardwood (from the genus *Prunus*) that darkens to a deep red over time and is highly valued. Magically, it has been thought of as an excellent wood for divination (see also "Willow"). Long associated with earthiness and environmentalism, cherry is the subject of Chekhov's play *The Cherry Orchard,* which tells of the demise of a beautiful cherry orchard, cut down to make way for a housing development.

+ *Ebony:* A tropical hardwood (from the genus *Diospyros*) that is especially heavy and usually almost black in color, which may explain its reputation as the most magical of all woods. It is related to the persimmon.

+ *Holly:* Holly wood (from the genus *Ilex*) is a white hardwood that comes from tall trees, a variety related to the small evergreen shrubs used to celebrate Christmas (the name comes from the word "holy"). Long used in Celtic regions, holly is known to have the magical powers of protection, purity, and strength, making it a good fit for Harry Potter's wand, which was made from holly.

+ *Hornbeam:* From the genus *Carpinus* of the birch family, hornbeam is a very hard, almost white wood that is often used when strength is a necessity as with the handles of fine tools. In fact, hornbeam is so hard that it's difficult to work with, so crafting a wand of hornbeam is no easy task.

+ *Mahogany:* Mahogany is a tropical tree of the genus *Swietenia* that is characterized by its dark, reddish-brown color. It is an expensive wood that is used when durability is called for, such as in furniture and boat-making. The wand of James Potter, Harry's father, was made of mahogany.

+ *Maple:* A tree from the genus *Acer*, this light-colored hardwood has distinctive leaves that can vary from golden to deep red in autumn; the sap is used to make maple syrup. Although most people think of maple wood as a blond—sometimes almost peach—color, maple woods can be plain and light or wildly marked and darker golden.

+ *Oak:* Oak trees, which bear acorns, are from the genus *Quercus* and produce a hardwood that yields a dark, golden wood. Mythological stories associate the oak tree with strength (oak trees were sacred to Zeus); it is no wonder that the half-giant Hagrid used a wand made of oak. The Celts revered oak trees and considered oak groves to be sacred places; in fact, the word *druid*, which refers to the poets, priests, fortunetellers, divinators, and other magicians of the Celtic world, literally means "oak-wise." Folktales from Wales also feature oak trees, which are considered extremely magical.

+ *Rosewood:* Rosewood (from the genus *Dalbergia*) is a tropical hardwood that sometimes smells just like a rose; its dark reddish-black wood can be almost purple. Pianos are often made of rosewood, which has a feminine quality that's often associated with beauty.

+ *Vine wood:* Hermione Granger's wand is made of vine wood, which is listed in old Celtic tree calendars as the wood associated with either August or September (Hermione's birthday month). However, vine wood does not exist in today's world, at least not any longer, so it was never placed in a particular genus.

Tourist Tip

To experience an outstanding variety of tree species (including several of the best wand trees) in one place, visit the University of British Columbia Botanical Gardens in Vancouver. This spectacular tourist attraction—a must-see if you're ever in British Columbia, Canada—is organized into separate gardens and forests that specialize in plants from around the world, most of which thrive in Vancouver's mild climate. Information is available at www.ubcbotanicalgarden.org.

+ *Willow:* Willow trees are from the genus *Salix* and generally have narrow leaves and flexible branches. One variety, the weeping willow, has branches so flexible that they bend all the way back down to the ground. Biblically, the willow is a symbol of sorrow associated with the Jews' exile in Babylon. Such trees have long been thought of as enchanted—when one ventures under the canopy of a weeping willow, interesting events are sure to happen. Northern European peoples associated willow rods with magical powers, and it is likely that the words "witch" and "wicked" are derived from "willow." Willow, like cherry, is known to be an excellent wood to use for divination. Harry's mother, Lily, had a wand made from willow, as does Harry's best friend, Ron.

+ *Yew:* An evergreen from the genus *Taxus* with red cones, yew is commonly used to make archer's bows because of its elasticity. Yew trees may live to be several thousand years old; thus, it makes sense that Lord Voldemort's wand is made of yew.

A Wand's Special Ingredients

Although the hair or feather of nearly any magical creature can act as the core of a wand, the three used most commonly by expert wand-maker Mr. Ollivander (see Chapter 7) are unicorn hair, phoenix feather, and dragon heartstring.

+ *Unicorn hair:* A unicorn is a one-horned animal (the Latin *unicornus* literally means "one horn") that otherwise resembles a horse. The horn of the unicorn was thought by the Greeks and Romans to have the power to heal deadly poisons; the hairs of this animal often go into the wands of wizards.

+ *Phoenix tail feather:* The phoenix is a large, magnificent, long-lived bird that, as it is dying, bursts into flames and is reborn from the ashes. For this reason, Egyptians (and many subsequent peoples) associated the phoenix with immortality. Fawkes, a phoenix kept by Hogwarts' Headmaster Dumbledore, donated two tail feathers to two wands—one went into the wand of Lord Voldemort, who believed he could achieve immortality, and the other to Harry Potter. For this reason, their two wands—and, therefore, their two persons—are inextricably linked.

+ *Dragon heartstring:* Dragons, large serpents whose name is derived from the Latin for snake (*draco*), are well represented throughout both mythology and literature. Chinese mythology (and later, Japanese culture) recognized dragons as gods of nature; the Greeks and Romans saw both potential for evil and potential for good. Early Christians saw dragons as inherently evil, however, and their reputation has remained as such today. Dragons also figure prominently in fairy tales and folk tales (with young men fighting them to save the subjugated princess) and more recent literature, particularly fantasy literature. Perhaps the two best known stories are Tolkien's *The Hobbit*, in which Smaug, the dragon, is the nemesis of the dwarves; and Michael Paolini's *Eragon*, in which dragon riders and their counterparts are the most powerful and revered of all nobility. Heartstrings, by the way, are the tendons and nerves that protect the heart.

Dressing the Part: Robes, Cloaks, and Hats

Most wizards dress in long, flowing, plain robes, similar to what U.S. judges still wear today, and rather like the robes of priests or monks, but not cinched at the waist.

Robes, made from a variety of materials, come in all colors, and can match the wearer's tastes, personality, or color preferences, or can show a particular affiliation, such as a school, house (a subdivision within a school), or team.

In school, at work, and even around the house, wizards wear their everyday robes (called work robes), often black and always floor-length (unless the wizard in question has had a growth spurt and hasn't yet purchased new robes). For ceremonies, celebrations, balls, and other special events, wizards wear dress robes in a variety of colors.

As has been true throughout history, in the wizarding world, the materials used in robes are drawn from geographic markers. Mediterranean wizards wear silk robes; wizards from cold climates wear fur, wool, and other warmth-retaining fabrics. In colder weather, wizards also wear long cloaks (that is, a long coat that wraps around the body and fastens near the neck but may not have actual sleeves) that either match or complement their robes. At Hogwarts, cloaks must be black with silver fastenings. Hats—generally black (although they can match one's robes) and pointed—may be worn during formal occasions, but rarely at any other time.

One other type of cloak—and one that's a rare find among wizards—is an invisibility cloak. When worn, others cannot see any part of your body under the cloak, so if you pull the cloak over your head and your feet are still covered, you'll be completely invisible. And you can even bring your friends along for the ride, as long as they, too, fit entirely under the cloak. An invisibility cloak has strikingly similar abilities as the One Ring in Tolkien's *The Hobbit* and *The Lord of the Rings*, but the Ring is, at least in the short term, easier to use than an invisibility cloak, because your entire body becomes invisible the moment you put the ring on—no worrying about your feet being seen, the cloak coming off your shoulders, and whatnot. But the Ring has the downside of drawing you ever closer to a major source of evil in the world, so there's that *tiny* issue of losing your soul and forever altering the world's balance of power between good and evil. Details, details. Either way, though, no matter how you make yourself invisible, someone can still bump into you and feel your corporeal being, and you still leave footsteps in snow, dirt, or ash.

As in nearly all cultures, personal wealth determines the style, fit, and quality of fabric used to make robes. Styles change ever-so-slightly from year to year, but wealthier wizards keep up with those trends, as well as using fine, beautiful, flowing fabrics for their robes. Wizards with less money to spend on their wardrobes will tend to be seen in ill-fitting, out-of-style robes made with courser fabrics and in less distinct colors.

Wizards throughout literature have always worn long robes and/or cloaks. Although Tolkien called what Gandalf wore a grey (and later white) "cloak," the garment's description appears to be more robelike than cloaklike. Gandalf also nearly always sported a tall, pointed blue hat—but he also traveled nearly constantly, and travelers have long worn hats wherever they go.

Sure, the long robe and pointy hat are dead giveaways for any wizard, but underneath, those in the wizarding world are the same as anyone else. Literally, they dress just the same—many wizards, especially young wizards, wear jeans, sweatshirts, and trainers (tennis shoes) under those robes.

King's English

Bowler hats, also called derbies, are very British, and although not as common in the wizarding world as a pointed hat, bowler hats are sometimes worn by Ministry officials. If you've ever seen a picture of Winston Churchill out in public in winter, you probably saw him in a bowler hat. A bowler hat comes exclusively in black and has a narrow brim. Another British type of hat, a balaclava, is a ski mask commonly used by bank robbers. In the cold winter months in Hogsmeade, a balaclava is a must.

Quills, Ink, and Parchment

Wizards are not early adoptors when it comes to technology, so you don't see any ATM cards, cellphones, MP3 players, or laptops among the wizarding set. But really, when you can use magic, do you really need high technology?

Two modern conveniences that would likely come in handy among wizards writing papers, taking notes, writing out shopping lists, and the like are the lowly, low-tech pen and paper. Not only do wizards *not* take notes on laptops, they don't even take notes with a ballpoint pen and pad of paper! Instead, wizards use a quill, dipped in ink, to write on parchment paper.

+ A quill is a feather of a bird that, when dipped in ink, is used for writing. Unlike modern pens, quills tend to be quite long and beautiful, especially one from a large, attractive bird, like that of an eagle. Imaginative wizards have come up with all manner of high-tech quills, including those that ink themselves, magically check spelling, correct any errors, and even derive the correct answer on exams. Smart-Answer, Auto-Answer, and Self-Correcting quills are, of course, banned during examinations. A Quick-Quotes Quill, used during a lecture or conversation, takes notes automatically, leaving the wizard to concentrate on the discussion at hand.

+ Black ink comes in bottles, into which a quill is dipped before writing on a parchment. This process can be rather messy, with ink bottles spilling, wet ink getting on one's hands or clothes, and ink bottles smashing when a book bag is accidentally dropped.

+ Parchment replaced Egyptian/Greek/Roman papyrus, which had been made by soaking the papyrus plant and drying it in thin sheets. When papyrus became inefficient as a tableau, parchment, made from the skin of an animal (usually sheep or goat), came into favor. Paper, which is used the world over by nonwizards, is made from wood pulp. Whereas paper comes in set sizes (generally 8½ by 11 inches) parchment comes in long rolls that are a bit difficult to manage—the parchment tends to roll up on you as you're writing, which can smear the ink. Unlike flat pieces of paper that stack and file neatly, rolls of parchment are also difficult to store.

Other Magical Gadgets

Although wizards don't embrace Muggle technology, they are not immune to the lure of gadgets. However, magical gadgets tend to be less about convenience and time-savings—as are most Muggle gadgets—and more about digging a little deeper into the depths of a wizard's magical powers. In this section, you discover just a few of the many magical gadgets available in the wizarding world.

Harmless (or Practically Harmless) Gadgets and Inventions

Some wizard gadgets are practically kidstuff—fun inventions that make life a little simpler or more exciting. And although a few of the gadgets listed here could, conceivably, be used for evil, in the wizarding world, they tend to be thought of as harmless. (For gags and inventions that are related to food, see Chapter 7.) Note than none of these clever gadgets has been given an especially creative name; these inventions are likely meant to appeal to younger children.

+ *Lunascope:* We don't know many details about this gadget, except that it's a silver instrument responsible for a revolutionary advance in astronomy by replacing moon charts (what we can assume are moon phase charts).

+ *Omnioculars:* A cross between binoculars and TiVo, Omnioculars look a lot like binoculars, but they can also slow down action, replay it, do a play-by-play, and so on. *Ocular* relates to the eyes, and *omni* means "all" or "everywhere."

+ *Put-Outer:* A Put-Outer, although not the most creatively named object in the wizarding world, has an important function, especially if you have nefarious purposes. A Put-Outer looks like a cigarette lighter, but when aimed at a streetlight (and, possibly, other lights as well), it steals the light and stores it. The streetlight thus goes out until the light is restored by the Put-Outer.

+ *Revealer:* An eraser that reveals secret ink written on what appears to be a blank page. This is the equivalent to the old homemade invisible-ink trick of revealing lemon-juice-based words by exposing them to a heat source.

+ *Remembrall:* The equivalent of a Muggle tying string around one finger, a Remembrall (remember-ball) reminds you of something you've forgotten. This smoky glass ball is roughly the size of a marble shooter; if you forget something important, the smoke inside the ball turns bright red.

+ *Spellotape:* From the British product Sellotape (the UK's equivalent to Scotch tape), Spellotape is a tape wizards use to mend books, wands, and the like. It's used so often that it's the wizarding equivalent of duct tape.

+ *Vanishing Cabinet:* Although the name may lead you to believe that the cabinet itself vanishes (if, for example, a classmate you didn't like was coming over to borrow your best sweater, you could temporarily make your cabinet of clothes disappear), that's not what a Vanishing Cabinet is at all. Instead, anything that's put *into* a Vanishing Cabinet— whether your best sweater or a person— disappears. The object (or person) is not made invisible; instead, it is transported elsewhere, often for days or weeks.

> ### KING'S ENGLISH
>
> If you met a Muggle who claimed he was in possession of a Dark Detector, you might think he was a little crazy, right? Well, if you lived in Great Britain, you wouldn't say he was "crazy," you'd say he was mental. He hadn't "gone round the bend"; he had gone round the twist.

+ *Wizard penknife:* The Swiss Army knife of the wizarding world, this penknife can unlock any locked door and undo even the most tangled of knots. The first is a little scary, what with the power that comes with undoing any lock; the second is quite convenient, especially if you've ever had your iPod's earbuds all in a wad.

Mirrors and Glasses

Mirrors and glasses have great power in the wizarding world:

+ *Foe-Glass:* This mirror reveals when enemies are nearby. A Foe-Glass (a glass that allows you to see your foes) shows figures moving about, all rather skulky and shadowy. When an enemy comes clearly into focus, he is close indeed.

+ *Mirror of Erised:* This massive mirror—perhaps only one of which exists in the wizarding world—shows you exactly what you desire ("Erised" is "desire" spelled backward). In fact, the inscription on the mirror, *Erised stra ehru oyt ube cafru oyt on wohsi*, proclaims "I show not your face but your heart's desire" when spelled backward. It does not show the future, but rather what you wish the present to be and/or what you hope the future will be.

+ *Talking mirrors:* As in *Snow White*, some mirrors in the wizarding world talk to the people who look into them.

+ *Two-way mirrors:* Like cell phones with a live video feed, two-way mirrors allow two wizards to talk to and see each other. Each must possess one of the mirrors, and both must be alive—two-way mirrors do not extend beyond death.

Objects That Give Advice

When Mr. Weasley's daughter, Ginny, narrowly escapes death in her first year at Hogwarts, he quips sound advice: "Never trust anything

that can think for itself if you can't see where it keeps its brain."
Wise words.

The objects in this section appear to be thinking for themselves—or, at
least, dispensing advice—yet we can't see where they keep their brains.
Still, the greater wizarding community does heed the words of these two
objects.

+ *The Goblet of Fire:* This cup is reminiscent of the Holy Grail: large;
carved from wood; and humble in its design. The Holy Grail,
reportedly the cup from which Jesus drank during the Last Supper,
has been the subject of countless stories, books, and movies,
from *Monty Python and the Holy Grail* to *Indiana Jones and the Last
Crusade* to *The Da Vinci Code.* Although precious, it is not known to
dispense advice of any kind. The Goblet of Fire, on the other hand,
is filled with flames, out of which pop the names of three wizards
who will join in the Triwizard Tournament (although, in one year,
the goblet was tricked into issuing a fourth name). The wizards
chosen by the Goblet are bound to complete the tournament—no
changes of heart are allowed after the names are announced.

+ *The Sorting Hat:* The Sorting Hat isn't much to look at, but oh,
what it can do! Old, torn, and not-so-clean, the Sorting Hat is
pulled out for the Sorting Ceremony at the beginning of each
school year at Hogwarts. After singing a song, the hat is placed
on the head of each new student, deciding in which house each
student will live. Sometimes the Sorting Hat makes decisions
quickly; other times, it mulls the choice carefully. When the
Sorting Hat is unsure of where to place the student, the Hat can
even confer with the student in question.

Journeying Through Time

If you're going to be a wizard, for gosh sakes, you have to do a bit of time
travel! It's what every Muggle wishes for, although a number of movies—
from *Somewhere in Time* to *Back to the Future* to *Frequency*—have shown
us the perils of interfering with the natural flow of time. Of the two
gadgets wizards have for traveling in time, the first allows one to be
an observer only, without interrupting the events of that time, and the
other gives one an opportunity to redo events of the past.

+ *Pensieve:* A Pensieve is a stone basin (to picture this, think of a stone birdbath) into which one's thoughts can be placed for safekeeping. Yep—that's right: thoughts (in the form of silvery wisps) can, by using a wand, be taken from the brain and placed in the Pensieve. If you have too much on your mind or want to protect yourself against Legilimency (see Chapter 13), a Pensieve is the way to go. Unfortunately, anyone who ventures near the Pensieve can, by dipping his face into the thoughts swirling in the basin, relive those thoughts as a firsthand observer. In this way, someone else can experience your innermost (and, perhaps, most embarrassing) memories. This object is aptly named: to be pensive is to think deeply and seriously, often tinged with sadness or melancholy. This word is from the French *penser*, which means "to think." And a sieve is an object used to sift and separate.

+ *Time-Turner:* A time-turner can be nearly any size, but it always looks like an hourglass. Each complete twist of the hourglass turns back time one hour. However, if, back in time, the time-traveling you runs into the original you, the consequences could be terrifying, so it's important that the original you never see the time-traveling you. The exception, of course, is if you are using a Time-Turner regularly, in which case time-traveling you could probably wave to original you, and both would find it amusing. To cut down on all this confusion, the use of Time-Turners is regulated by the Ministry. All Time-Turners had been kept in the Time Room in the Department of Mysteries at the Ministry of Magic, but they were all destroyed in a particularly messy encounter between Dark Wizards and good.

Protection Against the Dark Arts

Dark Wizards do exist, and if one's wizarding skills aren't top-notch, gadgets can help. Whether escaping from a dicey situation, shielding yourself from hexes and charms, or trying to detect the presence of evil or lies, these gadgets do the trick. Just beware: Dark Detectors, the purpose of which is to alert you to the presence of a Dark Wizard, can be fooled by a powerful wizard.

+ *Peruvian Instant Darkness Powder:* This powder, when thrown, makes everything go pitch black, thus allowing good wizards to escape from bad, but also bad wizards to escape from good. That it is Peruvian is a play on Paddington Bear's origins in "deepest, darkest Peru." You can also use a Decoy Detonator to make a fast getaway—this ugly, loud gadget makes a noise in one direction (in other words, works as a decoy) while you escape in the other.

+ *Shield Hats, Shield Cloaks, Shield Gloves:* Although unable to shield against the Unforgivable Curses (see Chapter 12), these gadgets allow lesser charms, hexes, and jinxes to bounce off the wizard wearing them, and sometimes even bounce back to the hexing wizard! Sold at Weasleys' Wizard Wheezes (see Chapter 7).

+ *Secrecy Sensor:* A Secrecy Sensor looks like a squiggly TV antennae (called a television aerial among the Brits); it begins vibrating when it senses secrecy (telling a lie, evading the truth, or concealing an important piece of information). Used properly, a Secrecy Sensor can also tell you when a jinx, curse, or charm has been put on a person or object.

+ *Sneakoscope:* One of the coolest inventions in the wizarding world, a Sneakoscope (and its smaller cousin, a Pocket Sneakoscope) whistles or lights up whenever it encounters someone untrustworthy. (It is a type of Secrecy Sensor.) Think of how handy this would be anytime you buy a used car, go on a date, or try to find out who stole your baseball mitt.

Chapter 4

How Wizards Spend Their Days

In This Chapter

+ Doing housework the wizarding way

+ Spending and saving money

+ Getting the mail

+ Listening to tunes

+ Investing in artwork

+ Dining and dancing

Are you plagued with gnomes in the garden? Can't tell a Knut from a Galleon? Wondering why the eyes in that picture appear to be following you? Pondering whether to say "yes" to an offer of Cauldron Cakes and pumpkin juice? You've come to the right place. This chapter helps you sort out all the ways in which wizards spend their days.

Cooking, Housework, and Gardening

To the uninitiated, wizard housework might seem oxymoronic. After all, if you're a wizard, for goodness sake, you're not going to spend time cooking, cleaning, and gardening, are you? Of course not! You're going to use magic to do all of that, the same way Mary Poppins helped the children "clean" up their room by snapping her fingers, and then singing about a spoonful of sugar.

But, alas, we see no such logic in the wizarding world. True, there are improvements, such as self-peeling sprouts, but tangerines, for some reason, still need to be peeled. Dishes can be charmed to clean themselves, but housekeeping is still considered a full-time job. Even Mrs. Skower's All-Purpose Magical Mess Remover (that's Mrs. "Scour" to you) doesn't relieve wizards of the drudgery of household chores. Creatures must be cleaned out of the most inconvenient places (see Chapter 2 for more on these nuisances), dinner must be made (or house elves must be employed to cook), and the plates must be cleared away.

> ### KING'S ENGLISH
>
> After a long day of household chores, you may want to take a kip; that is, a nap.

And perhaps the biggest challenge faced by a domesticated wizard is the havoc wreaked by garden gnomes. No, not the garden gnome statues that graced American lawns for most of the 1970s and '80s, but a brilliant takeoff: tiny, live gnomes (old-looking, and with very large, bald heads) that burrow in lawns (thus ruining them) and have to be caught and tossed—literally, tossed into the air as far away as possible. *De-gnoming the garden* is, for wizard kids, the equivalent to mowing the yard or digging dandelions out from between the bricks. (See Chapter 2 for more on gnomes.)

Managing Money

Although you might think that wizards can simply conjure money out of thin air, it doesn't work that way. Like Muggles, some wizards are rich and some are poor, but most are staunchly in the middle class, working full-time jobs. Moneyed families tend to stay that way, but capitalism is alive and well, which means that any wizard can create a successful business.

The similarities stop there, however, because wizard money and banking are rather different from their counterparts in the Muggle world.

Spending the Cash

Wizards tend to use cash exclusively, which must be extremely inefficient, given that wizard money exists only in heavy coin form. Never has a wizard whipped out a credit or debit card.

Three coins make up the entire monetary system:

+ *Galleon:* This gold coin is the most valuable in the lot. A galleon was a large sailing ship, used for trading, in the fifteenth and six-teenth centuries.

+ *Sickle:* Seventeen of these silver coins equal one Galleon. A sickle is a crescent-shaped blade that's used to cut down weeds. The sickle also appeared on the crest of the former Soviet Union.

+ *Knut:* Twenty-nine of these bronze coins equal one Sickle. Knut (also called Canute the Great) was king of Denmark and Norway, and was the first Danish king of England.

So what does this mean? Wizards use tall ships, rounded blades, and Danish kings to purchase items? No, but the names all do relate to com-merce, politics, and power in some way—a large and impressive trading ship, a farm implement important to a huge agrarian nation, and an influential king whose power spanned several nations.

Banking on Wizards

Most wizards store their money in Gringotts Wizarding Bank, which is run by goblins. However, unlike in Muggle banks, the money doesn't appear to be invested or used to finance buildings or other projects; instead, the coins simply sit in vaults until they're needed. Vaults (at least the important ones) are protected not only by high-level charms but also by dragons, and because the vaults are located 100 miles beneath the streets of London, break-ins are rare.

TOURIST TIP

Although not by any means the largest bank in London, C. Hoare & Co. is the oldest surviving private bank in the city, located at 37 Fleet Street. Founded in 1672, the bank is still run by members of the Hoare family. It is said that literary figures Lord Byron and Jane Austen both banked at Hoare's. For information, visit www.hoaresbank.co.uk.

Literature has a long association with goblins, dragons, and money. In J.R.R. Tolkien's *The Hobbit*, goblins (called Orcs in *The Lord of the Rings*) and Wargs (wolves) were said to have fought the dwarves, elves, and humans in the Battle of the Five Armies. Why? Because the goblins wanted the dwarves' treasure. And it was Smaug, a dragon, who stole the dwarf treasure and used it as his bed—never spending it, but enjoying the shininess of the coins and jewels.

Just like Smaug, when Eustace turns into a dragon in C.S. Lewis's *The Voyage of the Dawn Treader*, he finds himself sleeping on a bed of treasure—money, jewels, and gold. In Ursula Le Guin's *The Wizard of Earthsea*, dragons sometimes attack people when searching for treasure. The literary link between dragons, goblins, and treasure is deep indeed.

Hobgoblins, another name for goblins, also appear far back in British folklore as short, hairy, ugly creatures who can be friendly and helpful, but can quickly turn mean and nasty. That folkloric tradition fits the wizarding world's goblins to a "T." Goblins and hobgoblins also appear in the *Spider-Man* comics, the Dungeons & Dragons game, and even in Shakespeare (Puck, in *A Midsummer's Night's Dream*, is a hobgoblin).

Receiving Mail

Technology is irrelevant to wizards—why use overnight delivery services, text-messaging, and e-mail when you can use magic? So a wizard's first choice for contacting other wizards is not through high-tech means but through the mail service, which travels via owl.

The Role of Owls

Owls, not carrier pigeons or hawks, are the bird of choice for wizards. In fact, a local post office is little more than an owlery.

The rationale behind using owls is a little murky, but a connection between owls and magic is well established. Magic tends to be practiced under the cover of darkness; owls are nocturnal creatures. The consistent hooting of an owl has long been associated, right or wrong, with impending death, especially the death of a child. The Greeks and Romans believed that witches could turn themselves into owls, and then feast on babies. In fact, in many cultures, owls have been believed to act as messengers for wizards and witches, just as they do in the magical world of Harry Potter. And in T.H. White's *The Once and Future King*, Merlin has an owl named Archimedes.

The advantage to using owls is that they work seven days a week, they can deliver messages just about anywhere in the world, and they can find the addressee even if no one is supposed to know where he or she is. The downside is that owls must be cared for, fed, and given treats, and they can be temperamental. In addition, cats, another highly magical creature, don't tend to get on well with owls.

Howlers

One particular type of mail is a Howler. A Howler looks like it could be a letter in a red envelope, but when you open the envelope you get Howled at by the sender. Ignoring it only makes the screaming worse. When all the screaming is over, the envelope erupts in flames and burns. Howlers are sent mostly by parents to rebuke their children.

The Wizarding Wireless Network (WWN)

Nothing like the World Wide Web (WWW), the WWN is basically a wizarding radio station, playing mostly music. A wireless in the wizarding world is not a cell phone, Palm, or Blackberry, but a radio, as in the term used to denote radios in the early 1900s. "Wireless" was short for wireless telegraphy—the beauty of radio was that, unlike the telegraph, it was completely wireless, operating on radio frequency instead of using wires that crisscrossed the nation, as the telegraph did.

Wizard musicians aren't any different from nonwizard musicians, except that the lyrics of songs relate to issues wizards can understand ("A Cauldron Full of Hot, Strong Love" or "You Charmed the Heart Right Out of Me"). Celestina Warbeck (from *celestial*, meaning "heavenly," and *warbler*, a bird known for its sweet songs) is one such wizard singer.

Perhaps the most famous wizard group is The Weird Sisters, a rock 'n' roll band that sport long hair and torn black robes and might be loosely named after Twisted Sister, a heavy metal band popular in the 1980s. Just as likely is that they are a reference to the three witches in Shakespeare's *Macbeth*. Although The Weird Sisters' instruments include the usual drums and guitars, band members also play the lute, the cello, and the bagpipes, which are all traditional Celtic instruments.

Photos and Artwork

That the subjects in photographs and paintings change in the wizard world—that is, that they are not static—may not come as a huge surprise. After all, many horror stories are predicated on the notion that the "eyes" of paintings are watching you and following your every move. Egyptians painted images in tombs in the hopes that the images would come alive and assist and guide the soul of the deceased. F. Scott Fitzgerald used the eyes of Doctor T.J. Eckleburg in *The Great Gatsby*, up on a huge billboard, as a metaphor for God watching us. And perhaps the best-known changing picture is the one in Oscar Wilde's *The Picture of Dorian Gray*. The picture ages and displays the scars of a man who has lived a cruel life, while the subject of the painting, Dorian Gray himself, never ages a day.

But wizard paintings don't just change subtly; they move about, sleep, talk, and even leave their paintings to visit other ones! They can, in fact, be most annoying. The characters in paintings are much like their original subjects—they have the same opinions, tendencies, and characteristics as they did while alive. The Fat Lady, the subject of a painting that guards the entrance to one of the Hogwarts houses, regularly gossips, takes naps while on duty, and is terrified when her painting is slashed. Photos, on the other hand, are like silent movies that replay every few seconds; photo subjects also tend not to talk or leave their frames, but they do wave and smile.

And in what is, perhaps, literature's best imitation of *Monty Python and the Holy Grail*, one Sir Cadogan, formerly of a hanging picture, leaves his painting to go on a quest, yelling insults like "Stand and fight, you yellow-bellied mongrels!" A real Sir Alexander Cadogan was Great Britain's representative to the United Nations just after World War II.

We see plenty of the opposite in literature and culture; that is, people stepping *into* paintings. C.S. Lewis's *The Voyage of the Dawn Treader* begins with the children falling into a painting. And much more recently, in the movie *What Dreams May Come*, Robin Williams goes into one of his wife's oil paintings.

Eating and Drinking

British wizards eat and party like any Brit without wizard abilities, with some exceptions:

+ *Butterbeer* is an entirely wizardly invention, and like any good magical concoction, it has powers beyond simply tasting good— it's a nonalcoholic (except to house elves) soft drink that makes the drinker feel all warm and toasty inside. It's butterscotchy, with a nice froth on top like root beer. So, it's a butterscotch root beer (hence, "butterbeer"). The bottle caps can be strung together in a necklace, but none of the cool kids would do that.

+ *Pumpkin juice* would be easy enough to make in the Muggle world, but only wizards have a taste for it. If you strained pumpkins, the juice would be incredibly thick, but watered down and with some added sugar, the juice would make a tasty—and healthy—beverage. The juice is usually served cold in a flagon, which is a container that has a handle, spout, and, sometimes, a lid. Pumpkins are prominent in the wizarding world, but that's not surprising, given the prominence of pumpkins in Halloween celebrations.

Magic Tale

Do the British celebrate Halloween? Yeah—they invented it! Held every October 31, the tradition started as Samhain (pronounced SOW-an) Eve, the traditional end of summer for the Celts. It was believed that the dead, joined by other supernatural beings, came back to mess with the minds of the living for one night. The Catholic Church renamed the holiday All Saints' Eve (the night before All Saints' Day), or All Hallows' Eve, which is how the current name, Halloween, originated. Sometimes called Mischief Night (a night of pranks and other mischief for which children weren't punished), today's British celebration looks just like the American version, including door-to-door trick-or-treating.

+ *Dandelion juice* doesn't sound nearly as appetizing as pumpkin juice, but the idea is the same: strain the juice from dandelion stems or flowers, add a bit of sugar, and create a tasty beverage. Dandelion, which means "lion's tooth," goes by many other names, including wild endive, swine snout, and cankerwort. Dandelion has traditionally been used to treat digestive complaints.

+ *Firewhiskey* is, presumably, a whiskey with an extra kick. Although school children don't usually partake, Chocolate Cauldrons, a popular treat, are chocolate confections with a touch of firewhiskey inside them. Whiskey was, of course, invented in the British Isles.

Magic Tale

Perhaps it's too much of a stretch, but Ogdens Old Firewhiskey may have been named for Ogden, Utah. When most people think of Utah, they think of Mormons and temperance, not of whiskey. But Ogden, one of the only non-Mormon cities in Utah, was once a classic Old West town, with saloons, brothels, dance halls, and opium dens along the length of its famous 25th Street.

+ *Cauldron Cakes* are pancakes, presumably cooked, somehow, in a cauldron.

+ *Ginger Newts* are cookies, probably a cross between a ginger snap and a Fig Newton.

Simple Meals

Most wizard meals are the same as any Brit would eat on a given day; although Muggles wouldn't have their food appear out of thin air (as it does at any feast), nor would it be made by house elves (as it is at Hogwarts). But in general, if you know British food, you know wizard food. Problem is, our friends on the other side of the pond have an entire language for food that's almost indecipherable to Americans. Here's a sampling of the British food and drink routinely eaten by Hogwarts' students:

KING'S ENGLISH

Students at Hogwarts often **queue** for dinner, which simply means that they get in line. Ask any American over 50 what "queue" means, and they'll know; an entire generation of Americans learned the word "queue" from the rock band The Who in the 1970s: "Every morning I get in the queue, to get on the bus that takes me to you." If they had said "get in the line," it would have been a tougher rhyme—and it wouldn't have sounded nearly as hip and British.

+ *Biscuit:* A cookie, usually bought and served in a tin (a round metal box with a lid). Biscuit can also mean a cracker, a bit like an American saltine, but denser and often served with cheese. Either way, British biscuits are nothing like American biscuits, which are flaky, unsweetened pastries often covered in gravy.

+ *Chipolatas:* Small pork sausages usually served at breakfast; what Americans might call "breakfast sausage" or even "cocktail sausage." Not to be confused with bangers, which are large sausages served as part of an afternoon or evening meal, usually with mashed potatoes (in a dish called bangers and mash).

+ *Crumpet:* Unsweetened cake that's cooked like a pancake, but taller and not as large in diameter as pancakes are. In truth, a crumpet tastes a bit like a moist American English muffin.

+ *Cuppa:* Cup of tea; British tea tastes very much like heated-up iced tea—very lemony and not very strong. Brits add cream and/or lemon to a cup of tea. And tea mugs tend to be small and proper, not the giant versions served at some American coffee houses. Don't confuse cuppa with the word tea, a term that is generally used to mean a small meal.

+ *Kippers:* Salt-cured (often smoked) dried fish; usually made from herring, which is a thick, oily fish with a mild, sweet flavor. Tastes somewhat like smoked salmon, but oilier.

+ *Mead:* A sweet wine made from honey and sometimes aged in oak barrels. Elderflower wine, another type of wine, is just as obscure, but it does exist in both England and the United States.

+   *Mince:* Another word for ground beef or other meat chopped up into tiny bits. See also mince pie in the following section.

+   *Pasty (PAST-ee):* Think of a pasty as a Hot Pocket meeting a pot pie; that is, a flaky crust that fully surrounds a rather dry filling of beef or chicken, potatoes, onions, and other ingredients. You either love 'em or hate 'em, and if you hate 'em, it's because they're too dry and plain. At Hogwarts, they serve a sweet pumpkin variety unheard of in the Muggle world.

Tourist Tip

If you're traveling to London and want to eat cheaply, load up on pasties. You won't find Pumpkin Pasties, but the beef, chicken, and other main-dish varieties are huge, super-filling, and only about $4 each. Dessert varieties are smaller and cheaper. Eating pasties every day wouldn't be the healthiest choice you could make, but in a city as expensive as London, it's a filling and inexpensive food choice. The British-based West Cornwall Pasty Company has kiosks located throughout Underground and train stations in London and sells over six million pasties each year.

+   *Porridge:* Crushed oats or oatmeal (and, occasionally, other grains) boiled in water and/or milk and usually served with sugar and cream. When made with oats, porridge is said to look and taste exactly like American oatmeal, although many Americans would beg to differ.

+   *Tripe:* Stomach of a cow or ox; not everyone has the courage to try this one, but Hogwarts' students seem to think it's a treat. The term is synonymous with codswollop, although no one uses that term to mean the food; codswollop, which is used extensively among Hogwarts' students and staff, means "hogwash"; you can probably think of other, less-printable synonyms.

+   *Yorkshire pudding:* A hearty dish that's like an American popover—a small, puffy muffin filled with sausage, roast beef, beans, and just about anything else. May be served with horseradish sauce and/or gravy.

Snacks and Sweets

Like any meal anywhere in the world, it's not complete until dessert is served. And the British are no different; in fact, the Brits are wild about their desserts and tend to ladle creams and custards on almost all of them.

Keep in mind, however, that England does not have a reputation for its food. At least, it doesn't have a *good* reputation for its food. If you want great food, you go to New York or Paris or even Tokyo—you don't go to London. That said, they do have interesting—and possibly even enticing—desserts and other treats. The ones that follow are routinely served in the wizarding world:

+ *Chocolate gateau: Gateau* is "cake" in French, but in England, it's more than cake … it's a super-rich cake. Hence chocolate gateau is a rich chocolate cake, served in slices with fresh cream. Marie Antoinette is reported to have said "Qu'ils mangent du gateau," which translates literally to "Let them eat cake," but she meant "Let them eat rich, dense, creamy cake." It's a subtle difference (regular old cake versus a buttery, rich cake) but one important to cake connoisseurs.

+ *Christmas pudding:* A plum cake or plum pudding served with a rich sauce. Often, there's a coin baked in it for luck. You either love this or you hate it, and most American kids hate it, because plum pudding isn't super-sweet.

+ *Meringue:* Meringue is simply egg whites and sugar, but the dessert called "meringue" usually begins with a meringue crust (like a pie crust but made of meringue) that's topped with fruit or other sweet fillings. Meringue cookies are becoming popular in the United States because they are fat-free, yet very sweet, treats.

+ *Mince:* A pie made of mincemeat filling—apples, raisins, suet (beef fat), and sometimes (although not usually these days) chopped meat. It's actually quite spicy and delicious and may be served cold with custard or clotted cream (in other words, any sweet, thick dairy product) or heated up and served with brandy butter.

+ *Peppermint humbugs:* Hard candy flavored with peppermint oil. Like a candy cane in the United States, but striped black and white instead of red and white.

+ *Pudding:* Pudding simply means "dessert." Don't think of American pudding, which is more like *custard* in England.

+ *Spotted dick:* No, really. I'm not making this up. This confection sounds terrible, but it's not bad. You start with suet, which is beef fat, rub that into flour and make it into a pudding, and then add dried fruit (usually currants, which is where the "spots" come from). Like most British desserts, it's served with custard.

+ *Toast and marmalade:* Toast and jam, except that marmalade is usually made with oranges. The Beatles made marmalade famous when they sang about "marmalade skies."

+ *Tart:* Like an individual pie; a crust is topped with fresh fruit, jam, cream, and/or custard, but if you top it with treacle (which is like maple syrup), it's treacle tart.

+ *Treacle:* Treacle is a syrupy topping, with a consistency something like corn syrup but usually made with molasses. Treacle fudge, then, is fudge made with treacle. Treacle pudding is a steamed pudding made with the syrupy topping. *Treacle tart* is a tart with treacle drizzled on it.

Magic Tale

In C.S. Lewis's *The Lion, the Witch and the Wardrobe,* the White Queen entices Edmund to betray his siblings with Turkish Delight (a British dessert that is never eaten in the wizarding world). In the story, Edmund goes through an entire box of Turkish Delight in no time flat. But if you try this confection, you may wonder why in the world Edmund would betray his siblings for that particular dessert. To understand what Turkish Delight is like, start with a sort of dense, chewy, not-so-sweet marshmallow, sort of like taffy. Now, top that with sprinkles, like the ones you might put on a cake: orange, chocolate, lemon, or a dozen other flavors. That's Turkish Delight. For my money, you'd need a lot more than that to turn your back on your brother and sisters.

✛   *Trifle:* A many-layered confection that begins with sponge cake (sometimes soaked in rum or other liqueur), then fruit, then cream, and so on. If you really want to be decadent, you forego the fruit layers. Rather like our strawberry shortcake, but the cake is much spongier and mushier.

Going Out: Grand Feasts and Balls

Wizards are big on feasts, and to a lesser extent, on balls (that is, dances), too. Welcoming feasts are common at British boarding schools, but they're not referred to as "feasts," nor are they major celebrations. Instead, at British boarding schools, they serve you dinner the first night, and that qualifies as the "welcoming feast."

But in the wizarding world, every opportunity for a celebration turns into a feast: the welcome at the beginning of the year; the celebration at the end of the year; and just about every holiday in between. You've got to imagine that it costs a lot of Galleons to keep Hogwarts flush with all those feasts!

Hogwarts opens each school year with a Welcoming Feast, where new students are sorted into their houses, and a Leaving Feast, where the Inter-House Championship is awarded to one of the four houses. See Chapter 8 for more on Hogwarts' houses. Whenever possible, the Great Hall is decorated splendidly, but in decidedly magical ways—in fact, the ceiling of the Great Hall can be charmed to reflect the outdoor sky, or any other color scheme, for that matter. Although the castle is old and dark, the staff always find ways to make the students feel at home.

During the winter holidays, to the delight of the headmaster, feasts usually include wizard crackers. A regular cracker is a British holiday tradition: a combination toy and gift, when you pull the cracker apart (it's roughly the size of a paper towel tube, or even a little smaller), it makes a loud "bang!" and then out spill small treats or even small, inexpensive gifts. (It is not uncommon, however, for British men proposing to their girlfriends near the holidays to put an engagement ring in a cracker.) Crackers are sort of the same idea as a piñata, but much smaller and with the added fun of noise.

Wizard crackers, on the other hand, don't make a charming "bang!" but go off like a cannon blast that ends with an explosion of blue smoke, filled with small treats or gifts. Those unaware of the difference between British and wizard crackers have been quite thoroughly frightened.

Wizard balls are celebrations of the senses. Bands perform, wizards put on their best dress robes (see Chapter 3), and everyone dances. As with American proms and balls, food isn't the focus; although food is served, no one thinks less of a ball if the meal isn't the tastiest they've ever had. But hire the wrong band, and the entire ball is ruined.

Balls have a long tradition in Europe, one that has continued in American culture. Dances, proms, cotillions, and balls are a requirement of teenage and young adult life, and nothing gets a young girl more in a ball frame of mind than the *Cinderella* fairy tale. It's an age-old sentiment: dress up any girl in the right clothes and shoes, with care given to her hair and makeup, and give her a well-furbished vehicle in which to ride, and she'll be transformed—so much so that she'll win herself a prince.

Chapter 5

Getting Around: Modes of Transportation

In This Chapter

+ Getting to Hogwarts and back

+ Balancing on a broomstick

+ Traveling through fire

+ Apparating and Disapparating

+ Using a Portkey for special events

+ Knowing what to do in an emergency

Traveling through the wizarding world offers no fewer options than traveling in any other world. Wizards can journey by air, by train, by bus, and even by car on occasion. But in the wizarding world, air travel will be aboard a broomstick, train travel is on a secret train that can be accessed only by crashing headlong into a brick wall, bus travel is a hair-raising experience, and car travel is either in deceptively expansive vehicles or in the illegal flying variety. In addition, wizards travel through a network of fireplaces, by learning to appear and disappear at will, and even by touching just one finger to an object of trash before being whisked off to a prearranged destination.

Riding the Hogwarts Express

Train travel is far more common in Great Britain than it is in the United States, so no one there would be surprised to discover that the chief method of traveling to Hogwarts School is by train. What might surprise them is that the Hogwarts Express is an old-fashioned steam train, not the streamlined, modern trains found across Europe, Japan, and the United States today.

TOURIST TIP

Kings Cross Station—admittedly, a rather dodgy area of London—is easily accessible from all of greater London via the Underground (the name for the subway). If you go there and follow the signs to Platforms 8, 9, and 10, a sign will eventually indicate that Platform 9 (a & b) goes to the right, and Platform 10 (a & b) goes to the left. At that intersection, the place wizards crash headlong into the brick wall—some enterprising person has posted a wooden sign that says "Platform 9¾."

As with Muggle trains, passengers board a train on a platform—a waiting area in a train station. What's unusual about the Hogwarts Express, however, is that the platform is not visible to Muggles—instead, partway between Platforms 9 and 10 (which Muggles can see and use), wizard school children run into the brick wall and emerge—magically!—onto Platform 9¾ on the other side. Only wizards are able to accomplish this feat.

Traveling by train can be a fantastic experience, especially if you're staying the night and have your own private sleeping berth. You can buy meals and snacks on the train (or, as with the Hogwarts Express, train personnel come around with a food cart from which you can buy snacks). The food on a train generally isn't great, the bathrooms and sleeping berths are tiny, and you may experience a lot of rocking, jerking, and whistle-blowing—all of which can keep you awake at night. But you're also able to take in the scenery without having to concentrate on driving, you have much more room to stretch out and more opportunities to walk around than in a bus or plane, and strangers tend to mingle while in the dining car or even in their seats, which gives you a chance to meet a variety of people. For information on train travel in North America, visit www.amtrak.com (United States) or www.viarail.ca (Canada).

KING'S ENGLISH

British trains have their own language: a train car, in England, is called a **carriage**. A food cart is called a **trolley**. And if you travel at all by train or subway in England, you'll hear train personnel reminding you to "mind the gap." That's the British equivalent to "watch your step"; the **gap** being that narrow strip of distance between the edge of the carriage and the platform.

Tried and True: Riding a Broom

Brooms in the wizarding world look much like brooms in the Muggle world—not like today's modern brooms made of vinyl and other plastics, but like the brooms of old, which were made with a nobby but polished solid-wood handle and a head of straw or similar material. The only difference is that the wizard variety have the key addition of a Flying Charm and, sometimes, a Braking Charm.

The wizard task of riding a broom is very much like riding a bicycle is for Muggles—children love to do it because of the freedom it affords them, and some continue the activity well into adulthood (using it as a means of transportation and/or exercise), while others drop it in favor of less demanding traveling methods. While perhaps not as physically exertive as riding a bike can be, broom riding is definitely a form of exercise, one at which some wizards excel.

Brooms are also a bit like Muggle horses, in that wizards have invented a hugely popular sport to play while on broomstick, much like polo is played on horseback. You'll learn more about Quidditch and other wizard games in Chapter 6.

Brooms are reliable, safe, fun, and relatively inexpensive, especially if bought used. Wizards arrive at their destinations a bit windblown, but not nearly as dirty as when they travel the Floo Network (described in the following section). Plus, broomstick-riding doesn't require the great skill that Apparition does, as you'll see later in this chapter. In fact, many witches and wizards choose to never become proficient at Apparating, and opt instead for traveling by broomstick and the Floo Network.

Models of brooms run the gamut; the most common models include the following, and several slower, less-glamorous brooms are not even worth mentioning. Keep in mind that, as with any technology, better and faster brooms are always being released.

+ *The Firebolt:* The pinnacle of broomsticks, both in terms of speed and precision; it's like riding a "bolt of fire."

+ *The Nimbus series:* This series of brooms takes its name from the Latin word *nimbus*, meaning "cloud" or "rain storm." This is why the dark gray clouds that promise a drenching rain are called "nimbus clouds." The term may also have links to *Dragon Ball*, a Japanese cartoon from the mid-1980s, in which the Flying Nimbus is a flying cloud that characters use for transportation. In that series, "Only the pure of heart can fly the Nimbus Cloud." This is certainly not the case with Nimbus broomsticks, because Draco Malfoy, a student at Hogwarts who is decidedly impure of heart, successfully rides a Nimbus Two-Thousand and One. The latest models include the Nimbus Two-Thousand and the Nimbus Two-Thousand and One.

> **MAGIC TALE**
>
> Detailed information about the history of brooms—especially racing brooms—is available in the minibook *Quidditch Through the Ages* by J.K. Rowling (writing as Kennilworthy Whisp).

+ *The Cleansweep series:* As the name implies, these are functional, non-fancy brooms that one might even be persuaded to use for (gasp!) cleaning.

Disadvantages to broom travel are many:

+ *Temperature:* Rides can be exceedingly cold, even in summertime, because wizards have to ride high enough in the atmosphere to limit the risk of being seen by Muggles.

+ *Exhaustion over the long haul:* Because it takes a good deal of balance (to stay on) and strength (to hang on), broom travel can be exhausting during long trips. Even on short trips, wizards arrive looking windblown and harried.

+ *Speed:* Because you have to physically travel the distance from place to place, traveling by broom is slower than Apparating, using the Floo Network, or traveling by Portkey (described later in this chapter), but on a Firebolt, at least, broom travel is pretty darned fast.

+ *Risk of being seen:* Wizards must take anti-Muggle precautions when traveling by broom, because they are easily seen. A witch or wizard riding a broom against a full moon is a surefire way to be seen by Muggles.

+ *Risk of bodily harm:* Getting knocked off the broom is always a risk: one simple Hurling Hex, and the poor wizard will be spinning through the air without a broomstick.

Traveling the Floo Network

Using Floo powder to travel from place to place is an inexpensive, fast mode of travel. You must, however, have a fireplace through which to travel. In fact, a flue (for which *Floo* is named) is a shaft built into a chimney that allows smoke, exhaust, and air to escape. It is also the name of a pipe that moves dangerous exhaust gases from an indoor fireplace or furnace to the outdoors.

Here's how traveling by the Floo Network happens for wizards:

1. You take a tiny bit of Floo powder and throw it into the fire in the fireplace.

2. The fire turns green and the flames extend quite high.

3. Keeping your elbows tucked in, shutting your eyes, and staying as still as possible, you step into the fire and clearly shout the name of your destination.

4. You're spun toward your destination amidst a loud roar and a blur of the fireplaces you're passing.

5. You're deposited, rather dirty, to the fireplace at your destination.

Every wizard fireplace is on the Floo Network, which is policed by the Floo Regulation Panel, part of the Floo Network Office in the Department of Magical Transportation (see Chapter 14). Muggle fireplaces can also be accessed, but they are not usually connected to the Floo Network. And, these days, wizards have to be especially careful about boarded-up fireplaces, which cause obvious problems akin to what Santa goes through when fireplaces no longer allow for travel.

The major disadvantage of the Floo Network is that travelers are usually covered in soot by the time they reach their destinations. The experience is far from pleasant, because Floo travelers usually swallow some of the ashy powder and feel queasy during the ride. In addition, unless the wizard succinctly and correctly pronounces the name of the place he's headed, he could wind up in a dark and dangerous place, such as Knockturn Alley, which is not far from Diagon Alley, but is a world apart (see Chapter 7). Wizards also must find a container in which to store their Floo powder, such as a flowerpot.

A distinct disadvantage is also that the network is watched carefully. For a wizard trying to avoid detection, travel by the Floo Network is a dangerous route. As you're spinning through the fire, anyone can reach into a fireplace and grab you—a decided disadvantage if you're trying to stay under the radar.

TOURIST TIP

Tudor architecture (1500–1575) ushered in the age of fireplaces in English homes. Although indoor fires had been used before this era, most indoor "fireplaces" were dangerous open fires, with the smoke escaping through a small hole in the roof. Tudor-style homes featured brick or stone fireplaces and chimneys, which dramatically decreased the risk of indoor fires. To see some of the best Tudor architecture in England, including dozens of magnificent fireplaces, visit Hampton Court Palace (outside of London; www.hrp.org.uk/HamptonCourtPalace) and Knole House (near Sevenoaks, Kent; www.nationaltrust.org.uk/main/w-vh/w-visits/w-findaplace/w-knole).

Mastering the Art of Apparition

Apparition involves both Apparating (appearing out of thin air) and Disapparating (disappearing into thin air). The skill is a difficult one to attain, which is why the Department of Magical Transportation requires practitioners to apply for a license and pass a test. (And even very proficient wizards don't always pass the test the first time around.) Difficulty in learning to Apparate is also why many witches and wizards choose to travel by other methods, chiefly broom and Floo powder.

In the English language, apparition refers to unexpected or extraordinary appearances or to the act of appearing. Specifically, an apparition refers to the appearance of a strange, ghostly figure. Anyone who watches wizards Apparate and Disapparate would surely think they were seeing ghosts, so the name makes sense!

The primary advantages to Apparition are that it's free, clean, and instantaneous: wizards arrive at their destinations the second after they Disapparate. They also don't have to suffer the cold winds of broom travel or the discomfort of traveling the Floo Network. However, those under 17 years old are not allowed to Apparate on their own (similar to obtaining a driver's license in the United States). However, side-along Apparition is possible—that is, a person unable to Apparate can travel alongside one who can, just like a side-car on a motorcycle—but this is usually used only in emergencies.

Disadvantages to Apparition are threefold:

+ *Avoiding Hogwarts:* Wizards cannot Apparate or Disapparate within the grounds of Hogwarts School of Witchcraft and Wizardry because of tight security surrounding the school.

+ *Startling others:* Apparition tends to startle others who are nearby as wizards Disapparate and Apparate. One's appearance (or disappearance) is accompanied by a loud crack, but the crack is just as startling as the wizard's sudden appearance (or disappearance). Unexpectedly appearing or disappearing next to someone is considered bad form.

+ *Splinching:* Witches and wizards who are not proficient in Apparition may splinch themselves; that is, they leave part of themselves behind. Not only is the wizard unable to move either way (back to where he came or where he was headed), but Muggles usually see any body parts left behind. The Accidental Magic Reversal Squad must usually be called in to rectify the situation; wizards who splinch themselves are heavily fined.

Finding a Portkey

Portkeys (*keys* to trans*port*ing) are objects that, when touched, transport witches and wizards from one predetermined location to another. Portkeys are overlooked objects that appear to be trash: examples include a boot or shoe, a discarded newspaper, empty cans or bottles (although wizards have to be careful about using those in areas that strongly encourage recycling), and an old punctured football (that would be a soccer ball to Americans).

Portkeys are always set up by the Ministry of Magic; unauthorized Portkeys are nearly impossible to arrange, although powerful wizards have certainly been successful at doing so.

The process works like this:

1.   A group of wizards meets at a predetermined site, at a predetermined time.

2.   As the time approaches, all those present lay at least one finger on the Portkey.

3.   At the appointed time, the wizards are pulled, along with the Portkey, toward another predetermined site in a twirling, stomach-jerking motion.

4.   Used Portkeys are then collected at the destination site.

Experienced wizards can remain standing when they arrive at the destination, but the uninitiated often tumble to the ground. All who travel this way find themselves looking quite windblown.

Traveling via Portkey is a once-in-a-while experience for witches and wizards, because Portkeys are arranged only for significant events, such as the Quidditch World Cup (see Chapter 6), in which massive numbers of wizards, including children who are too young to Apparate, are traveling to a single location.

Summoning the Knight Bus

The Knight Bus is an emergency mode of transportation for a wizard who finds herself stranded and unable to travel in any other way. She simply extends her wand, and the triple-decker purple bus appears in a blinding light and with a loud bang. Triple-decker buses don't exist in England (although double-decker ones do!), nor do any British buses offer featherbeds to passengers, as the Knight Bus does. The windows are curtained to give privacy, so many passengers wear pajamas and slippers during the ride.

One advantage of the Knight Bus is that it travels quite fast. One disadvantage is that it, well, travels quite fast! Drinks spill, the beds move about, and travelers may find themselves rather carsick. The bus appears to be about to collide with objects (trees, lampposts, other vehicles) at a high rate of speed, but just in the nick of time, the objects move out of the way until the bus passes. At each stop, the driver slams on the brakes.

Aside from the obvious discomfort, another disadvantage is that the Knight Bus cannot be summoned unless someone is absolutely stranded. Like the knights in King Arthur's time, this bus should be one's last option, but it is one to be counted on, if needed. After all, given all that questing the knights did, they couldn't be spending all their time rescuing damsels in distress. But when a damsel has used up all her other options, the knight will certainly take time out of his questing schedule to do a bit of rescuing. In the wizarding world, both males and females can call on the Knight Bus.

Chapter 6

The Sporting Life: Quidditch, Chess, and Other Games

In This Chapter

+ Discovering the greatest wizard sport

+ Playing the game of kings with ornery pieces

+ Dueling the new-fashioned way

+ Joining a Gobstone club

+ Playing Exploding Snap

+ Trading cards, wizard-style

Wizards like a good game as much as anyone, but if *you* had the ability to fly on a broomstick or get advice from your chess pieces, would you settle for ordinary soccer or regular chess? Balderdash! You'd use your magical powers to devise sports and games that match—and challenge—your abilities. This chapter explores the best wizarding games, including the greatest wizarding sport on earth: Quidditch.

Quidditch

Quidditch has been played in the magical world for over 800 years and is wildly popular, both to play as a pick-up sport in the backyard and to watch. Like the Fédération Internationale de Football Association (FIFA) that governs British football (soccer), the International Association of Quidditch governs the sport and sponsors a World Cup match roughly every two years.

King's English

In Great Britain, a **pitch** is an area of land used as a grassy playing field. In addition, soccer is called **football** in England. Put it all together, and what Americans would call a soccer field is what Brits would call a football pitch.

According to *Quidditch Through the Ages* by J.K. Rowling (writing as Kennilworthy Whisp), the term *Quidditch* comes from the field in which the first game was played—Queerditch Marsh—in the eleventh century. However, others have postulated that the name comes from a combination of the names of the three balls used in the game: **Qu**affle, Blu**d**ger, and Golden Sn**itch.**

Balls and Players

Quidditch has been called a combination of polo, basketball, and British football (soccer). Like basketball, a ball is thrown back and forth among players as they aim, ultimately, to put the ball through a hoop, and points are earned by getting the ball through a hoop. However, three such hoops exist on each end of the field, and they're fifty feet in the air. Like polo, players ride on something instead of running with their own feet, but in Quidditch, that "something" is a broom.

But Quidditch is most like British football. Like soccer, Quidditch is played on a grassy pitch. A bright-red ball the size of a soccer ball (called a Quaffle) is passed among players called Chasers, and is eventually thrown through a goalpost (also called a hoop) for 10 points. (In soccer, the ball goes through the goal posts for 1 point.) Each team has three Chasers, and their only job is to control the Quaffle and score with it. (Note that, by definition, a *chaser* is a person who hunts or pursues, just as Chasers pursue control of the Quaffle.)

Also like soccer, each team has one Keeper, who is nearly identical to a goaltender. (Note that the definition of *keeper* is a guardian or protector; in Quidditch, the Keeper protects the goal so that the opposing team cannot score.) Finally, like soccer's quadrennial World Cup, Quidditch national teams gather every few years for World Cup competition.

Unique aspects of Quidditch that are unlike soccer (and unlike any other Muggle sport) are as follows:

+ *The Golden Snitch:* The Golden Snitch is a bright-gold ball, roughly the size of a walnut, that flies with fluttering silver wings. Catching the Golden Snitch, which is terribly difficult given its size and speed, earns a team 150 points and automatically ends the game. *Snitch*, by definition, means to steal something small; the Seeker must steal the Golden Snitch in order to win the game. Note that, in early forms of the game, a Golden Snidget, a tiny bird, was used in the game until the practice was outlawed. The name of this ball is thus based on the bird's name.

+ *Seeker:* One Seeker per team spends the entire game seeking out (that is, searching for) the Golden Snitch. Seekers are the smallest, fastest players on the team.

+ *Bludgers:* Bludgers are small, black, heavy balls, a little smaller than the Quaffle, that aim themselves at players and try to knock them off their brooms. (Beaters can also aim Bludgers at certain players.) A similar word, *bludgeon*, refers to a short club with a thick, heavy or loaded end; Bludgers in Quidditch are thick, heavy, loaded balls that are batted away with thick, heavy, wooden bats.

+ *Beaters:* Two Beaters per team carry heavy bats and try to protect the other players on the team by batting away Bludgers when they come near (or, more accurately, trying to bat Bludgers away from their own players and *toward* opposing players). In hunting terminology, a *beater* is a person who drives game out from under cover. And the flat bats Beaters use are reminiscent of bats used in cricket, a British game much like American baseball.

Perhaps one of the greatest differences between soccer and Quidditch is that, in Quidditch, boys and girls play together on teams. Girls, in fact, often make excellent seekers, given their smaller size.

Cheering for Your Favorite Team

Quidditch fans can cheer for national squads, such as Irish International, during the World Cup, and can support house teams at Hogwarts, where each house is trying to win the annual Inter-House Quidditch Cup.

Players who excel at Hogwarts or on the national squad can join the professional ranks after finishing their studies at Hogwarts. Three professional Quidditch teams have ties to popular football (that is, soccer) teams and to British Muggle towns:

+ *Chudley Cannons:* The town of Chudleigh is located near Devon, England. In Australia, the Oakleigh Cannons is a perennial powerhouse football (soccer) team.

+ *Wimbourne Wasps:* A town called Wimborne is in Dorset County, as are Wimborne Minster and Wimborne St. Giles. The London Wasps is a popular rugby team (a game similar to American football, but with a larger ball and without helmets and all the padding).

+ *Puddlemere United:* Puddletown also lies in Dorset County, about twenty miles from the town of Mere. The team likely gets its name from a merging of these two towns. In addition, Britain's most popular football (soccer) team is Manchester United.

West Ham United Football Club also garners fierce loyalty, both in the Muggle world and the wizarding world. Surprised that wizards cheer for Muggle soccer players? Keep in mind that many Hogwarts students lived as and among Muggles for their first eleven years, before being invited to Hogwarts.

Chess, Wizard-Style

Wizard chess follows the same rules as everyday chess, and every piece has the same name and guidelines about moving around the board. In both Muggle and wizard versions, putting the king into checkmate wins the game.

However, as with many seemingly static objects, in the wizarding world, wizard chess pieces talk, move, and have their own personalities.

Chess sets likely do a brisk business in the wizarding world, because the most unusual hallmark of wizard chess is that the pieces beat up on each other when they take another piece. Instead of the player removing the taken piece (as happens in Muggle chess), the prevailing chess piece whacks the piece that was taken. But the pieces do mend back together. So chess sets take quite a beating, but a well-worn set offers the benefit of pieces being on friendly terms with the owner of the set.

In addition, the chess pieces offer advice, give opinions on what they believe to be bad moves, and try to talk their way out of being sacrificed for the good of the game. It's like having a bunch of loud-mouthed cowards shouting out their advice on the game.

Dueling with Wands

Dueling with wands is not much like dueling with swords or pistols. It involves standing face to face with another wizard, wands out, and seeing who can bark out the fastest, most effective, most disarming (and, if necessary, most pain-inducing) spell, charm, hex, or curse. (See Chapter 12 for a list of blistering curses that will have your opponent crying "uncle" in no time.)

Wizards would no more parry with wands as nonwizards would fence with plastic spoons, because a wand's strength is in its ability to deliver spells, not in the actual strength of the wood. Wands can and do break, a condition that either renders the wand useless or causes spells to backfire. So you'll hear no clinking of wands during a wizard duel, just lots of spells being yelled among younger wizards (older wizards who have mastered nonverbal spells will utter no sounds at all), with the one who strikes first—and hardest—winning the battle.

Magic Tale

In *Eragon* and *Eldest*, the first two books in the *Inheritance* fantasy series by Christopher Paolini, dueling practice plays a large role both in the lives of dragon riders (who are much like Hogwarts students in that they must learn all the rules of the use of magic) and among elves (themselves very magical). Both riders and elves practice swordplay by applying a spell to the sword blade that blunts and dulls it. In this way, two swordsmen can practice as if in a real battle, but without causing any harm to the opponent.

But wizard duels do share some similarities with the more traditional forms of dueling. Like medieval duels and those conducted regularly between roughly 1500 to the mid-1900s, wizard duels may begin with a formal bow by both contestants, who must pay careful attention, during the duel, to their techniques in gripping and using their wands. Likewise, in both fencing and shooting practice, much time is spent perfecting technique.

But rarely is dueling about niceties. Although dueling with wands is a sport, it can also be a personal war, just as with sword and pistol duels. In this way, although young wizards compete in a Dueling Club at Hogwarts (started by Professor Gilderoy Lockhart), if the two wizards in the duel have a personal grudge, the match will soon turn ugly. Compare a fencing match, which is played with blunt-ended rapiers, to a true sword duel, such as those in *The Lord of the Rings* and *The Chronicles of Narnia*, and you see few niceties or emphasis on technique—just Lord Aragorn or High King Peter slicing off an opponent's head.

The difference between dueling for sport and dueling for real is as striking as the difference between a professional boxing match and a street brawl: people often get killed in the latter. Think of the quick-draw pistol duels in the Old West, where the idea was to kill the other shooter with the first shot, not to rack up points so that your team wins the dueling match.

In this way, true wizard duels—that is, those played not for sport but those that are a fight for life and death—are intense battles. Dark Wizards strike fast and hard, giving their opponents little time to duck and cover, deflect the curse, or yell a countercurse. And Dark Wizards in a duel do not hesitate to use the Unforgivable Curses (see Chapter 12), which lead to torture, death, or complete control by the Dark Wizard so that his opponent must do his bidding.

⊛   MAGIC TALE

The Ministry of Magic is intensely anti-dueling, as have been most government agencies through the ages. Governments ban dueling because the practice flouts the law by searching for justice in a duel rather than in a court of law. Historically, Muggle duels nearly always began with an offense, whether real or perceived. The offender was then not channeled through the legal system but instead challenged to a duel by the offended, who chose the rules: fight to first blood; fight to serious wounding; or fight to death. *West Side Story* depicts a modern-day duel, as Bernardo and Riff fight each other, ostensibly to serious wounding, over perceived offenses. Unfortunately, they end up fighting to the death.

Like duels with swords, wizard duels require the assignment of a second, a trusted representative assigned by each dueler, who assures that the contest is a fair fight.

Gobstones

Gobstones is a game played often by wizard children that's similar to marbles. However, because few people are expert in marble-playing anymore, here's the lowdown on the nonwizard version:

1. You first draw a small-ish circle on the ground, as well as a larger circle a few feet outside the first.

2. All players agree on how many ⅝-inch marbles to put in the circle and, standing behind the larger circle, players throw that number of marbles into the smaller circle.

3. Taking turns, each player throws, tosses, rolls, or barely flicks a ¾-inch shooter (also called a taw or boss; a large marble) into the circle, with the goal of hitting the smaller marbles that are in the circle hard enough to knock them out of the circle.

4. As with chess, if you knock a marble out of the circle, you get to keep it. If you're playing "keepsies," you get to keep the marble indefinitely. If you're playing "fair," you give back all captured marbles at the end of the game.

5. If your shooter stays in the small circle, your turn is over. If the shooter comes out of the small circle, you get to take another turn.

King's English

In Britain, **gob** means to spit; thus, **gobstones** are spitting stones. The word is borrowed from a Scottish Gaelic word that means beak or mouth (the area from which spit originates). **Shut your gob** is the British version of shut up, and **gobsmacked** or **gob-struck** refers to being astonished.

6.   The player with the most marbles at the end of the game wins.

If you've ever played bocce, the two games are almost identical, except that bocce is like marbles on steroids; the balls used are much larger.

Gobstones, then, is a wizard version of marbles, in which the player whose marble is knocked out of the circle not only loses the marble, but also gets shot with a nasty liquid by the marbles that remain in the circle.

Exploding Snap

Snap is a common children's card game, played by two or more players. The entire deck of cards is dealt, but players do not look at their cards; instead, each player turns a card face up on a pile in the center of the table. When a player turns up a card of the same color and value (such as two red fives or two black kings), the first player to yell "snap" gets all the cards in the pile. The first player to hold all the cards in the deck wins the game.

Turning this simple children's game on its ear, wizards play Exploding Snap. Admittedly, the wizard version is initially easier to play than regular Snap, because the dealer doesn't have to shuffle; wizards use self-shuffling cards. But after the cards are dealt, Exploding Snap has an entirely different personality than Snap, because the cards might explode at any moment. Naturally, the possibility of exploding cards creates a more strategic game than regular Snap.

Another use for exploding cards is to build a house of cards, which, what with the occasional destruction wrought by explosion, is akin to building a house of cards on an active fault line or during a category-five hurricane.

Trading Cards

More of a collectible than a game, trading cards with moving pictures of famous wizards come in packages with Chocolate Frogs. Wizard kids collect and trade the famous wizard cards, either among friends or through common-room notice boards, in the same way that Muggle children collect an Alex Rodriguez or Derek Jeter baseball cards. The most popular cards include:

+ Agrippa
+ Circe
+ Cliodna
+ Albus Dumbledore
+ Nicolas Flamel
+ Alberic Grunnion
+ Hengist of Woodcroft
+ Merlin
+ Morgana
+ Paracelsus
+ Ptolemy

Chapter 1 shares the accomplishments of these famous wizards, witches, sorceresses, Druids, alchemists, and astronomers.

Chocolate Frogs are both challenging (they tend to jump away) and healthy (staving off the effects of dementors—see Chapter 15); they are considered excellent holiday and get-well gifts.

As with sports stars, the wizards on trading cards tend to value the tribute to them. When Albus Dumbledore faces losing his many titles and privileges within the wizarding community, as well as facing the possibility of a jail sentence in Azkaban, he jokes that they can take away anything, but not his place on Chocolate Frog cards!

Part 3

Magical Places

This part gives you details on London's wizard gathering spot—Diagon Alley—including the background on stores, bars, the hospital, and other locations. Then, you travel to Hogwarts School and Hogsmeade, England's only all-wizard town, and sample what the headmaster and shop owners offer there. Finally, you take a quick flight around the globe to visit two additional wizarding schools.

Chapter 7

Where the Witches Go in London

In This Chapter

+ Visiting Diagon Alley: wizard central

+ Avoiding Knockturn Alley and its Dark Wizards

+ Finding the Ministry of Magic in London

+ Making a trip to the wizard hospital

London is a city of nearly 8 million Muggles, but it's also the place for wizards to mingle, shop, take care of Ministry business, and cure what ails them. Although carefully hidden, the magical sections of London are, indeed, wizard hotspots. Come on in, and enjoy the wizarding sights and sounds of London!

Diagon Alley

Diagon Alley, deep in the heart of London, has to be one of the most creative destinations ever invented. Located off Charing Cross Road—which is, arguably, the best street for bookstores (both new and used) in the entire world, the alley is accessible only to wizards and to Muggles who are there with their wizard children. The alley travels "diagonally" from Charing Cross (hence, the name), and can be reached on foot, by vehicle, or through any of the wizard means of transportation (see Chapter 5). If arriving on foot, visitors must first enter the Leaky Cauldron, and proceed through that pub to the alley.

Gateway to the Alley: The Leaky Cauldron

It is not surprising that J.K. Rowling would use a pub as a gateway to the magical world within London. After all, Great Britain is teeming with pubs—in fact, Edinburgh, Scotland, has more pubs per square mile than any other city in Europe. And Limerick, Ireland, boasts a place called the Cauldron Pub.

The Leaky Cauldron, unlike its Muggle counterparts throughout Great Britain, is a wizard-only gathering place (it's both a pub and an inn; the inn faces Charing Cross Road). It isn't much to look at—small and shabby—but it's the entrance to one of the coolest wizard shopping centers on the planet, if you know how to get through the brick wall behind the pub. Tap the bricks with your wand and they slide back, revealing a street of shops and window-shopping wizards.

KING'S ENGLISH

English **pubs** (which are short for "public houses") can be the equivalent of American bars, or they can also be inns, offering both a bar and hotellike rooms for the night. Rooms at pubs may have individual baths (as do most hotels in the United States) or may share a bath with one or even several other guests. An **inn** may or may not have a bar that serves alcoholic beverages, but it always offers meals. A **hotel** or **private hotel** generally will *not* have a bar on the premises, although it will usually serve breakfast. And, finally, a **brewpub** is a pub in which beer is brewed onsite.

Cauldron Shop

Just inside the entrance to Diagon Alley, the first store is a cauldron shop that sells—you guessed it—cauldrons of all sizes and materials. Some even have magical spells put on them to make the stirring process easier. Cauldrons, which are bulbous pots, usually with a collapsible handle, are used to brew potions by boiling herbs, pieces of magical animals, and other objects.

Cauldrons have been used since the dawn of time. The witches in *Macbeth* are, perhaps, the most well-known witch-users of cauldrons, but cauldrons have been in existence for millennia as simple cookpots. From the Latin *caldarium*, for "hot bath," cauldrons were staples of kitchens. The Celts may have been the first to use cauldrons to makes stews and soups, hammering them from silver. Later, cast copper and bronze were used, and finally, cast iron was introduced. Rowling names all but cast iron as materials, and she also mentions pewter (required at Hogwarts) and gold, which were, perhaps, used in some areas of the world, where those metals were prolific.

Cauldrons are also used in each Olympic Games; the Olympic torch, which is often carried throughout the country in the weeks or months before the games begin, lights the Olympic Cauldron and, thus, marks the beginning of the games.

The cauldron shop on Diagon Alley remains nameless in the novels, but Warner Brothers found it necessary to name this shop in the DVD tour given in the *Harry Potter and the Chamber of Secrets* movie. In that tour, it is called Pottager's Cauldron Shop. A pottager is a small garden, arranged in a grid pattern, that incorporates flowers, herbs, and vegetables, all items that would be used in stews and soups made in cauldrons.

Apothecary

Like apothecaries in Muggle history, this store is the equivalent of a modern pharmacy. Today, pharmacies sell "potions" that have already been brewed, but apothecaries of the past sold the ingredients only; it was up to the purchasers to brew the medicines themselves. (This is kind of like buying the ingredients for dinner at the grocery store, versus getting take-out that's already made for you.) The wizard Apothecary sells herbs, roots, and powders (see Chapter 10 for more on uses of specific herbs), as well as other wizard tools of the trade, like the feathers, eyes, horns, claws, livers, spleens, and dung of various animals.

Although this store is called only "the Apothecary" throughout the *Harry Potter* novels, in *The Sorcerer's Stone* movie, it is referred to as Slug & Jiggers Apothecary. A slug is both a unit of mass (equal to 32.2 pounds) and another name for a shot (as in, "a slug of whiskey"), while a jigger is both a unit of volume (equal to 1.5 fluid ounces) and a quantity of alcohol (as in, "a jigger of whiskey"). Such precise measures fit perfectly with the apothecary business.

Eeylops Owl Emporium

Because owls are both pets and an important communication link in the wizarding world, nearly every wizard household has an owl. And with that many owls in that many wizarding homes, owl-specific stores are bound to pop up. Eeylops Owl Emporium sells all sorts of owls (tawny, screech, barn, brown, and snowy), as well as owl treats and nuts.

Eeylops is a tougher word to translate than one might imagine. However, *ops* is the Greek word for "eye" (think Cyclops, which is *ops* combined with the Greek *kyklos*, meaning "circle or wheel"). So, in this case, *eeyl* likely means big, wide, or night, relating to the qualities of owls. I say "likely" because modern Greek does not show such a word. Ancient Greek, however, included the word *ey*, which meant "well," and that translation (well-eyed) makes sense: owls have particularly good vision; in fact, being called "owl-eyed" refers to one's exceptional eyesight.

Florean Fortescue's Ice Cream Parlor

One of the favorite hangouts of wizard kids, this ice cream shop used to serve ice cream of all varieties and flavors to wizards sitting at small tables placed on the sidewalk. As Chapter 4 points out, food is one of the few areas of crossover between Muggles and wizards—with the exception of some candies and other magical treats, food choices among the two groups are surprisingly similar, and ice cream is no exception.

The parlor owner's first name, Florean, is reminiscent of fluorine, the chemical element commonly called fluoride that's added to water to counteract the effects of sugary ice cream and keep teeth from decaying. With no dentists in the wizarding world, perhaps Mr. Florean Fortescue's ice cream contains a product that's similar to cavity-fighting fluorine. Fortescue is a common last name in both the wizard and Muggle worlds. A Mr. Fortescue was a headmaster at Hogwarts, and Sir John Fortescue wrote the history of the British Army; Father Adrian Fortescue was a notable writer, and Fortescue Arms is a bed & breakfast in South Devon.

Mr. Fortescue, the parlor owner, was, by the look of things, "dragged off" in Harry's sixth year. The general assumption is that he was, in some way, connected with the Dark Arts, and was kidnapped or killed (but check out Chapter 16 for the final word). This doesn't mean he was a Dark Wizard, but that he had some connection, and that connection went south. Think of Dark Wizards like the Mob; you cross them, and they'll break your thumbs, *capice?*

Flourish and Blotts

Flourish and Blotts, the wizard bookstore, is aptly named: a "flourish" is writing in an ornamental style, while a "blot" is a spot or stain from spilled ink.

Like any good Muggle bookstore, Flourish and Blotts is full of shelves of books stacked nearly to the ceiling and offers periodic book signings by favorite authors. The difference between a Muggle bookstore and Flourish and Blotts is in the books themselves: they may be leather-bound or covered in silk; book sizes range from so tiny you can barely see them to so huge you can barely lift them; the books may be written in strange languages or with runes (see Chapter 13) or may even be blank; the books may bite, snap at, or even fight you; and the titles are all appropriate to the wizarding world alone, with topics ranging from Hogwarts textbooks to books for the wizard general public, including self-help, how-to, autobiographies, histories, and sports books. Compare this to the usual offerings at Muggle bookstores: hardcopy or paperback; all virtually the same size; in the (rather mundane) categories of fiction, children's, self-help, cooking, travel, business, and so on. If visiting a Muggle bookstore is a delightful experience (as it is to most book lovers), just imagine what walking through such a store must be like!

Gambol and Japes Wizarding Joke Shop

Until the appearance of Weasleys' Wizard Wheezes (discussed later in this chapter), Gambol and Japes Wizarding Joke Shop used to be the only place to buy irreverent, fun, jokey items in Diagon Alley (although Zonko's Joke Shop in the city of Hogsmeade also sells such items). In spite of recent competition, however, from Weasleys' Wizard Wheezes, discussed later in this chapter, Gambol and Japes is still the best place to find Dr. Filibuster's Fabulous Wet-Start, No-Heat Fireworks. What are they? Fireworks, of course, but with a twist. You can start them when wet, and they can't burn you. What could be better?

This shop's name couldn't be more appropriate: to "gambol" means to frolic, jump about, and skip, while to "jape" means to jest, joke, or play tricks. And that's exactly what you'll find at this shop—items that are excellent for joking and playing tricks, as well as items that encourage jumping about and skipping.

Magic Tale

To take a tour of Diagon Alley, check out the companion DVD to the movie *Harry Potter and the Chamber of Secrets.* Although getting into the video production of the alley takes a bit of (potentially frustrating) work, because you have to click the bricks in the proper order (just remember, "three up ... two across"), once inside, you get to virtually visit several shops.

Madam Malkin's Robes for All Occasions

Madam Malkin's is *the* place to go for wizard clothing of all sorts. Whether you're a witch looking for everyday robes or a wizard shopping for dress robes, you'll find them all here. As Chapter 3 points out, most wizards wear black for every day; Hogwarts uniform robes are also black. But when dressing up (or for the wizard who doesn't mind spending a little more for everyday wear), robes appear in whatever color you can imagine.

As at any high-quality clothing store, Malkin's robes are fitted and altered, as needed, by Madam Malkin herself. The owner's name is a bit of a mystery, however; "malkin" means "a sloppy, slovenly (and even slutty!) woman." The proprietor of this clothing store would hardly be described as "slovenly." Secondary meanings are a mop, a scarecrow, a rabbit, and a cat, none of which makes any more sense than the first meaning. If Madam Malkin were at all unkind or unpleasant, her name could be seen to mean "bad folk," from the French *mal* (bad) and the English *kin* (family; relatives; kinfolk). But aside from being rather nervous, the shopkeeper has displayed only a happy, pleasant demeanor. On the other hand, Malkin is a common surname in England; perhaps that is the only meaning we can glean from the name.

Twilfitt and Tatting's is the alternate store to Madam Malkin's, selling the same sorts of goods, and perhaps even a higher quality of robes and cloaks. It may or may not be located on Diagon Alley. "Twill" is a way of weaving cloth; "fit" refers to how clothing drapes on a body; and "tatting" is a fine lace. Thus, Twilfitt and Tatting's name certainly reflects its contents.

Like Muggle resale shops and Goodwill or Salvation Army stores, another place to shop for robes and cloaks is in a second-hand shop. Owners of robes resell them as they outgrow them, which makes for great bargains. In Rowling's novels, shopping at second-hand stores is a matter of deep embarrassment; among American teenagers in the Muggle world, not so much, given the current popularity of Salvation Army and Goodwill Stores as a means of expanding one's wardrobe.

Ollivanders

Ollivanders may be the most intriguing store in Diagon Alley. Makers of fine wands since 382 B.C.E., the small, dusty store has nothing but boxes upon boxes of wands, stacked one on top of the other. Some wands, without a doubt, have been sitting there, gathering dust, for 2,300 years!

Mr. Ollivander, the proprietor of the store and, we assume, something like the ninety-fifth generation of Ollivander to work there, has an incredible memory for wands. He remembers every wand he ever sold: the wood used; the length; the flexibility of it; and the magical core of it.

Mr. Ollivander is a tough nut to crack. Is he evil, or is he good? Did he join the Dark Side when Voldemort publicly returned in Harry's sixth year, or was he kidnapped or otherwise dragged off, causing his store to close? Harry certainly gets a strange vibe from Mr. Ollivander when the man talks about Voldemort. And Harry Potter fans have pointed out that "Ollivander" is an anagram for "an evil lord." On the other hand, *ander* is German for "other," and *oliv* is German for "olive," so the man's name could mean "other olive." Of course, that wouldn't make a whole lot of sense. Check out Chapter 16 for the last word on Mr. Ollivander.

Other Shops

Two other shops are named in the DVD tour of Diagon Alley (on the companion DVD to *The Chamber of Secrets* movie) that are not named in the book:

+ *Wiseacres Wizard Supplies:* From the vague name, this store could sell nearly anything, but it likely sells the telescopes, globes, and other instruments Harry sees in a shop window his first time in Diagon Alley. A "wiseacre," which is derived from the word "wise," refers to a person who claims to be knowledgeable about everything (but isn't).

+ *Scribulous Writing Instruments:* This would likely be a shop quite similar to Scrivenshaft's Quill Shop (see Chapter 8), selling quills, ink, and parchment. "Scribulous" is from the word "scribe," referring to a clerk or secretary; the word "scribe" derives from the Latin *scribo,* which means to write or compose. This shop is also called Scribulous Everchanging Inks in *The Sorcerer's Stone* movie.

Knockturn Alley

Knockturn Alley, likely a play on the word "nocturnal" (dark; nighttime), is a side street off Diagon Alley that sells only objects related to the Dark Arts. The name may also draw on the idea of being knocked around (mistreated) and living a life of hard-knocks (difficulties). The largest store in Knockturn Alley is Borgin and Burkes, named for the two shopkeepers.

+ Caractacus Burke is reportedly named after Irishman William Burke, a bizarre serial killer who, with help from a partner, murdered dozens of people in Edinburgh in the late 1820s, selling the bodies as fresh cadavers to a local medical school. (Caractacus, too, was a real person, a British hero who tried to fend off Roman invaders; it was also the first name of the character played by Dick Van Dyke in the movie *Chitty Chitty Bang Bang*).

+ Mr. Borgin's etymology is not clear; records show a ship named the *Borgin* was shipwrecked near Greenland in the mid-1900s, although why that particular ship would have been relevant is not clear.

Having trouble distinguishing "traditional" wizard supplies from "Dark" wizard products? No one would blame you, as a "unicorn horn" or "beetle eye" could, to the uninitiated, sound like something only bad wizards would use, but they're both sold at the above-board, not-Dark Apothecary. The distinction seems to be that, in Knockturn Alley, animal products are alive (that is, you'll find live spiders in Knockturn Alley versus the spleen of a dead animal in Diagon Alley proper). In addition, products that are dead, come from—or, at least, are made to look like they come from—humans, such as human fingernails or a human hand that grabs you and won't let go. This distinction does make some sense, because, even in the Muggle world, torturing live animals is illegal, and cooking up human livers will get you either thrown in jail or sent to a mental institution, but using the meat from an animal in your stew is perfectly acceptable. It's a fine line between good and evil, but it's one that exists in both the Muggle and wizarding worlds.

A few other items are also sold in these stores:

+ Masks are all the rage in Knockturn Alley. Similar to the Ku Klux Klan in generations past, Dark Wizards prefer to hide their identities when they set off for a night of evildoing.

+ Instruments of torture also make their appearance in Knockturn Alley stores. And given how many wizards mysteriously disappear by Harry's sixth year, chances are, those instruments are being put to use in hideous ways.

+ Poisons and cursed items (often jewelry of some kind) are sold here, presumably to slip to Muggles or to your sworn wizard enemies.

Most of the items sold in Knockturn stores appear, according to Ministry law, to be legal to sell but illegal to possess.

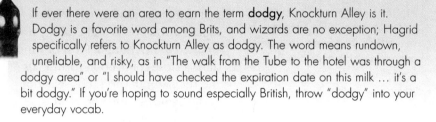

The Ministry of Magic

Hidden deep under London, the Ministry of Magic is where wizarding rules are made and punishment is meted out. It is the governing body for all British wizards. Chapter 14 discusses the Ministry in detail, so this section won't get into those particulars, but just know that it's located in central London, hidden well underground. The entrance from the Muggle world is in an old-fashioned, bright-red telephone booth, which are classic London landmarks—even with the abundance of cell phones (or mobiles, as the Brits call them), those old-style telephone booths still abound throughout the city.

St. Mungo's Hospital for Magical Maladies and Injuries

St. Mungo's is the place to go if magic has harmed a wizard in any way. Healers attempt to reverse the damage done, although some are more successful in the healing arts than others.

Rowling's creative genius is in the details, and her description of St. Mungo's is no different, specifically in the floor guide of the hospital in *Harry Potter and the Order of the Phoenix*.

TOURIST TIP

The Church of Saint Mungo in Glasgow, Scotland, was founded in 1850, but it was built on the site of a wooden church St. Mungo built in the early 600s. If you venture to Glasgow, you can visit the church, hear mass, and see a statue of St. Mungo. Even better, without even leaving your home, you can hear podcasts from the church by visiting www.saintmungo.org and clicking on "Podcasts."

But where does the name originate? Does "mungo," in this case, refer to its dictionary definition: scraps left over from making milled wool? Nah. Believe it or not, Rowling did not make up "St. Mungo." That's a real person—the patron saint of Glasgow, no less!—but "Mungo" was a nickname that meant "dear one." (His real name was Kentigern.) Various supernatural events and healing are credited to St. Mungo, most of which show a close connection to animals and the natural world. His selection as the namesake for a hospital is, therefore, quite appropriate!

Getting In: Purge and Dowse Ltd.

To get to St. Mungo's, wizards travel to a department store called Purge and Dowse Ltd. For years, a sign in the store has read, "Closed for Refurbishment," and one suspects that will always be the case, because the location is so convenient for wizards. Leaning in close to the glass, wizards simply tell the dummy in the window who they're planning to visit or what their medical condition is, and they tumble through. Voila! They are in St. Mungo's. And Muggles don't even notice the disappearing wizards.

Purge and Dowse Ltd. couldn't be more aptly named: to "purge" is to cleanse or get rid of impurities (and this applies to any hospital worth its salt); to "dowse" (an alternate spelling of "douse") is to immerse in or drench with liquid, as you would do with soapy water on a nasty wound.

Wizard Healers and Nurses

Wizard healers wear lime-green robes with an emblem of a crossed wand and bone on their chests. They're not surgeons (wizards don't cut on each other), but they are exceptional wizards who have the skills to undo spells, cure illness, and repair the effects of accidents, poisons, and bites. There are, of course, some maladies for which there are no cures (the effects of the Unforgivable Curses, discussed in Chapter 12, and werewolf bites, discussed in Chapter 2, are examples). But wizards distrust Muggle surgery and try to avoid it.

In the lobby of St. Mungo's is a portrait of Dilys Derwent, who was both a healer at the hospital and headmistress of Hogwarts. Dilys is a Welsh name, meaning "genuine." Dilys is also the name of a prestigious award (the Dilys Award) given by the Independent Mystery Booksellers Association to the book(s) members most enjoyed selling throughout the year. The award is named for Dilys Winn, who founded the first mystery bookstore.

Derwent is actually a first name for boys, derived from the Old English name Derwin, which means "dear friend" or "gifted friend." That would make Dilys Derwent a genuine, gifted friend; quite appropriate for a reputable healer. The Derwent River exists in both North Yorkshire, England, and Tasmania, Australia (the Tasmanian river is named for the British one). And the Derwent Hospital in Tasmania, Australia, was the oldest mental hospital in Australia when it closed in 2001.

Chapter 8

Hogwarts School and Hogsmeade

In This Chapter

+ Getting the lowdown on Hogwarts School

+ Comparing the wizard school to British boarding schools

+ Understanding the houses within boarding schools

+ Reviewing common boarding-school curricula

+ Discussing forbidden forests

+ Visiting Hogsmeade, the only all-wizard city

Pigs (or hogs) and witches go way back. During the 1600s and 1700s, when witch hysteria peaked in the United States, the general public accepted without hesitation that witches flew through the air on the backs of rams or pigs; that witches were harming the pigs, cows, and crops of innocent neighbors; that a witch would steal a plump pig for a midday meal if she were passing by your farm; and that witches themselves had cloven hooves (a hoof split into two toes).

Witches were thought to have made a pact with the devil; it is not surprising, then, that pigs, goats, and rams (any animal with a cloven hoof) were thought to be Satanic. In the New Testament, Jesus sent demons into a herd of pigs, which then leapt to their deaths in a frenzy.

Hence we're given the names of two prominent places in the wizarding world: Hogwarts School and Hogsmeade, the only all-wizard town in England. "Hogwarts" is especially inventive because it also uses the imagery of warts, which is how we historically picture witches, with prominent warts on their chins or noses.

Hogwarts School of Witchcraft and Wizardry

Each year, the staff at Hogwarts School of Witchcraft and Wizardry selects a new class of potential students, drawing children from established wizarding families and Muggle children who show a penchant for wizardry. How the staff is aware of the talents of these children is unknown, but they just *know*, starting from the day children with wizard abilities are born.

Invited students are sent letters the summer after Level 6 in the British education system, which is the equivalent to fifth grade in the United States. Letters tell candidates that they have been admitted (no one *applies* to Hogwarts; you're either invited or you're not), and students have to appear on September 1, bringing with them the required robes (plus a cloak and a hat), equipment (such as a cauldron, telescope, scale, and phials), work gloves, books, and a wand. Students are also allowed to bring a pet, but the only allowable pets are owls, cats, toads, and rats.

Other than the unique class offerings, ghosts, magical creatures, secret rooms, talking portraits, moving staircases, and a variety of other oddities discussed in this chapter, Hogwarts is strikingly similar to British exclusive prep schools. Some such schools are boarding schools just like Hogwarts, where students and teachers live on the grounds for the school year; others are day schools, in which students return home each evening. The top-tier schools, however, are boarding schools.

Like Hogwarts, many British boarding schools divide into houses, which compete for annual inter-house prizes as Best House by earning points in athletic events, debate, artistic endeavors, and/or academic competitions; by good behavior; and by raising money for or spending time working with charitable organizations. Houses allow students of various ages to interact and feel camaraderie; something that happens in most U.S. schools only through athletic or artistic extracurriculars. Select professors serve as Head of House or Housemaster.

KING'S ENGLISH

British boarding schools are, oddly enough, called **public schools** in Great Britain. This terminology comes from the idea private schools accept all students from the general public who were willing to pay to attend, not just students from a small geographic area. The top four British public schools are Eton College, Harrow School, Charterhouse School, and Worksop College. Andover and Exeter are American equivalents.

British public schools often start students as young as age 3, working on rudimentary reading and writing. They enter Level 1 at around age 5 or 6, which is equivalent to the U.S. kindergarten. Although students are generally grouped into classes with other students who are the same age, they are sometimes allowed to progress at their own pace, regardless of age or class. Within classrooms, students are usually subgrouped by ability, with a specialized curriculum aimed at each group. The best girls' boarding schools admit students after Level 6 (or fifth grade); this is how Hogwarts admits students, but they admit both boys and girls at this age. Boys' schools generally begin later, after Level 8 (seventh grade).

As with British schools, Hogwarts has a headmaster or headmistress (sometimes called just a "Head" in British schools) who acts like a U.S. principal, but because most British public schools are boarding schools, Heads discipline 24/7 and know the students far better than do most principals.

British boarding schools usually assign the best and brightest students to act as Prefects, House Captains, and Head of School. The term *prefect* (a term used at Hogwarts) comes from the Latin *praefectus*, which means director, chief, or governor (*prae* means "put in front" or "put in charge"). In Hogwarts and other British boarding schools, prefects have great authority over other students, controlling and (sometimes) punishing students so that teachers can focus on their work. When a prefect is put in charge of an entire house, he or she may be called House Captain, a term not used at Hogwarts. The senior prefect is called the Head of School, or Head Boy/Head Girl, the latter of which is also used at Hogwarts.

Hogwarts students wear uniforms (in their case, black robes), as do all British boarding school students. The uniform varies, of course, but British students usually wear a blazer, pants or a skirt, a white shirt, and tie.

Hogwarts also has a prominent coat of arms, as do most British boarding schools:

+ Hogwarts: A lion, an eagle, a badger, and a snake (the four symbols of the four houses), surrounding an "H"

+ Eton: The French fleur de lys, three lilies, and a lion

+ Harrow: A lion and crossed arrows

+ Worksop: A silver cross with four lions

+ Charterhouse: A dog and several lilies surrounding the crest, which consists of three circles and three semi-circles

Getting into the top British boarding schools is a bit different than the magical "knowing" approach that the Hogwarts staff employs. Instead, young Brits take the Common Entrance Examinations (CEE), usually at age 11 for girls and age 13 for boys. Each school has it own requirements for CEE scores, which test English, math, science, geography, history, religion, and languages. Results of this exam may also determine which classes students take for their first two or three years at the school.

Hogwarts Four: The Houses

Grouping students into houses is a long tradition at the best British boarding schools. Houses have names (often, as is the case with Hogwarts, houses are named for founders, but also for headmasters and significant alumni), and the names are usually shortened to the first letter of the name, like "G" or "P." British houses, like those at Hogwarts, may have colors assigned to them, and students dress (in their ties or scarves) per their house colors.

The top British boarding schools all have numerous houses, which can either be actual "houses" (that is, separate structures on the school grounds) or may signify wings of the school in which students live (as is the case at Hogwarts).

+ Eton College educates over 1,200 boys, but the houses are small: 25 houses each consist of about 50 boys. Although it is not the most expensive school by any means, Eton is considered the best of the best.

MAGIC TALE

If you've heard of Eton College, perhaps that's because all of England's royal boys have been educated there. (And remember, Eton College is a high school, not a university.) Given how many young British girls hope to meet the princes of their generation, sending young princes to an all-boys school— away from all those girls—makes sense!

+ Worksop College, the smallest and newest of the elite British boarding schools (founded in 1890, when it was called St. Cuthbert's), has just under 500 students, ages 13 to 18. The school is split into seven houses. In addition to excellent test scores, Worksop is well-known for sports, especially field hockey (which the Brits call just "hockey") and cricket (something like American baseball, but played with a flat bat).

+ Harrow School is more than 400 years old and educates approximately 800 boys at any given time, split into 11 houses. Harrow is one of the most expensive boarding schools in Britain.

+ Charterhouse School is England's *most* expensive public school, and has 11 houses—seven new that, in the 1970s, joined the original four from the school's opening in 1611. Charterhouse admits only boys (about 400 of them) until Level 12 (the equivalent of eleventh grade; called the Sixth Form at many boarding schools), when girls (about 100 of them) are admitted, along with another 250 boys.

Of the top four British boarding schools, two are for boys only; Worksop alone is coeducational, and Charterhouse admits girls for only the last two years. Although Great Britain boasts many girls' boarding schools, not one all-girls school is considered even close to being in the same league as the top all-boys schools.

At Hogwarts, students are grouped into four houses, and they compete for the House Championship, which is awarded as a House Cup. The Hogwarts House Championship is earned, as at other boarding schools, through athletic competition, prowess in the classroom, and good behavior.

The Hogwarts houses (called the Hogwarts Four) are each named for the four founders of the school.

Magic Tale

Talking hats in literature are not common, but hats do have an important place in children's make-believe—think of what a child can do with a pirate's hat, magician's hat, cowboy hat, or firefighter's helmet. Several fairy tales are based on hats—invisible hats, magical hats, and multiplying hats. And don't forget that Dr. Seuss made his reputation on hats (*The 500 Hats of Bartholomew Cubbins* and *The Cat in the Hat*).

Students are sorted into houses with the help of the Sorting Hat (see Chapter 3). During the Sorting Ceremony, first-year students pull on the large hat (which usually dwarfs their small heads) while sitting on a stool in front of the student body. The hat then reads the mind of (and sometimes speaks to) the student, trying to discern the personality, gifts, and ambitions of each student.

Two noticeable differences exist between Hogwarts houses and the top British boarding schools. First, as a general rule, British boarding schools allow students to choose their own houses (which is why some houses are bigger than others). Students must be accepted by the House Master, and everyone understands that the House Master may not be the House Master the entire time that student is at the school. However, the House Master is the gatekeeper—the Sorting Hat of the Muggle world—taking applications from incoming students who would like to live in that particular house.

Second, houses in British schools do not have personalities; at least, the schools do not officially acknowledge that one house is more intelligent, while another is more athletic, for example. Houses at British boarding schools are supposed to be diverse groups that reflect the makeup of the student body at large. Hogwarts' houses, on the other hand, have distinct personalities that reflect those of the founders.

The Great Hall, Towers, Dungeons, and Other Common Areas

Hogwarts School is set in a castle, complete with towers, turrets, dungeons, on the banks of a lake. Like most castles (both those in real life and those in literature), it can be dark and cold, although eager house elves (see Chapter 2) keep the fires burning in common areas. Each house has its own section of the castle, and classrooms are either on the main floors, in dungeons, or in towers. There is also a library, overseen by Madam Irma Pince (from the French *pince-nez*, small glasses that pinched the nose instead of gaining stability by wrapping around the ears), which has both a Restricted Section (for which students must have special permission from professors) and an Invisibility Section, which, one presumes, is rather difficult to locate!

The Hogwarts Great Hall is patterned after the enormous halls in both British castles and castles throughout literature (think of the many great halls mentioned in J.R.R. Tolkien's *The Lord of the Rings* alone). The Great Hall has a bewitched ceiling that reflects the weather outside the castle. At the High Table sits the Hogwarts faculty; students sit at long tables—one for each house. The hall is usually decorated to match the season or other occasion; for some occasions, thousands of candles float magically above the tables.

Tourist Tip

A visit to Christ Church, one of the colleges at Oxford University, is an absolute must for Harry Potter fans. (Oxford, England, is a short day trip from London.) Christ Church's Great Hall, a grand area used for college functions, was used as the model for the Great Hall set in the Harry Potter movies, and various other college locations were used as well, including a staircase built in the 1500s. Visiting hours are from 9:00 A.M. to 4:30 P.M. daily. For more information, visit www.chch.ox.ac.uk, click on Visitor Information, and click on Harry Potter.

Students at Hogwarts are admitted to certain areas (house common rooms, the headmaster's office) by means of a portrait, painting, or statue, which demands a password from students, rather like the electronic passkeys used at many schools. Passwords at Hogwarts are changed every few weeks and, of course, some students have trouble remembering them. (These are the same students who can never remember their locker combinations in the Muggle world.) In addition, the numerous staircases at Hogwarts move periodically, which befuddles most first-year students. The way you came up (to a classroom, for example) may not be the way you go back down.

Although not widely discussed or even known about, a Marauder's Map of Hogwarts shows the location of every person in the school, allowing the student(s) in possession of the map to wander the school undetected by avoiding all teachers and staff. On the other hand, if a teacher is in possession of the map, students cannot wander the halls without getting caught. The Marauder's Map sees even a wizard who is wearing an invisibility cloak (see Chapter 3). A "marauder" is one who roves about in search of plunder, from the French *maraud*, meaning "vagabond" and "tomcat," both wandering beings, so this is a map for those seeking to roam around and probably up to no good!

Classes: From Arithmancy to Transfiguration

Where Hogwarts does differ radically from its British boarding school counterparts is in the curriculum. To illustrate just how different they are, consider that the National Curriculum of the UK includes the following topics:

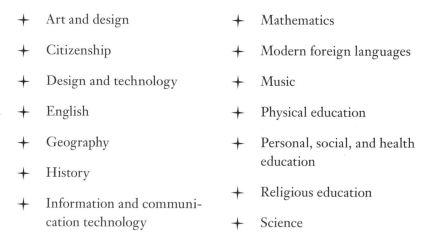

+ Art and design

+ Citizenship

+ Design and technology

+ English

+ Geography

+ History

+ Information and communication technology

+ Mathematics

+ Modern foreign languages

+ Music

+ Physical education

+ Personal, social, and health education

+ Religious education

+ Science

The list may be a bit more rigorous than most American public schools, but the curriculum is similar nonetheless to what American students study. Hogwarts even has a few classes that look like they could almost fit in:

+ *Ancient Runes:* In this class, students learn to understand the significance of runes, a 24-character alphabet that's further described in Chapter 13.

+ *Arthimancy:* Arithmancy comes from the Latin *arithmetica* (arithmatic) and the Greek- and Latin-derived suffix *–mancy* (divination). This field is better known in the Muggle world by its other name, "numerology," or deriving meaning from numbers. It is positioned as an incredibly difficult class, taught by Professor Vector ("vector" has multiple meanings in mathematics, all relating to a line denoting distance and magnitude). Professor Vector is also the name of one of the two professors in the Gryomite video game from the mid-1980s; a game J.K. Rowling could, conceivably, have played as a teenager or young adult.

+ *Astronomy:* Astronomy is, perhaps, the only Hogwarts class that is also taught at Muggle schools. It is taught by Professor Sinistra; "Sinistra" is, appropriately enough, a star in Ophiuchus, a large, faint constellation in the northern sky.

+ *Care of Magical Creatures:* This is the equivalent of a 4-H class teaching kids how to care for cows, goats, and horses. But instead, young wizards learn how to care for many of the creatures described in Chapter 2. Most Hogwarts students will never encounter such creatures; in fact, many of the creatures discussed in class are completely foreign to Hogwarts students.

Clearly, while British schools and Hogwarts differ in curriculum, a few similarities exist. At both Hogwarts and the top British boarding schools, students sometimes double classes; that is, the same class is taken back to back, in order to give students longer class periods in which to learn material. Many U.S. private schools also take this approach, as do some U.S. public schools that are utilizing block scheduling.

In addition, students at both Hogwarts and all the British boarding schools take exams partway through their schooling and again near the end. The first exam is called the General Certificate of Secondary Education (GCSE) in the Muggle world; Ordinary Wizarding Levels (O.W.L.s) in the wizarding world.

The GCSEs are usually taken after Level 11, which is the equivalent to tenth grade in the U.S. system, or roughly at 16 years of age. Some schools have students take the tests a year or two earlier, but regardless, the year in which exams are taken is usually called the Remove year. Following the Remove Year is either a year called the Fifth Form (if exams are taken earlier than Level 11) or the Sixth Form (if exams are taken at Level 11). The last year in school is usually called the Upper Sixth. Grades in the exams run from A* (A-star; the best) to B, C, D, E, F, and G (the worst). Failing completely means a grade of U (for unclassified).

Students who receive five or more A* to C grades are allowed to take A-level classes during the Sixth Form. A grade below C in English or math can result in retaking the exam or in leaving school to join the work-force, although that is extremely rare at the best boarding schools.

Likewise, O.W.L.s are given by the Wizarding Examinations Authority at the end of the fifth year (like the GCSE, usually at about age 16). O.W.L.s are spread out over two weeks; theory exams are given in the morning, while practice exams are in the afternoon. The exception is Astronomy, which is tested at night.

Grades are as follows:

+ O = Outstanding

+ E = Exceeds Expectations

+ A = Acceptable

+ P = Poor

+ D = Dreadful

+ T = Troll

As you may have guessed, a "T" is really, really bad, as if you have the intellect of a troll. Ouch. Like the GCSE, O.W.L. results guide students' last two years of coursework. Failure to achieve a passing grade in an area usually means that classes in that area are no longer available to students. At British boarding schools, after the GCSE, students begin to specialize, moving from O (ordinary) subject levels to A (advanced) levels.

Another similarity between O.W.L.s and the GCSE is that students can try crazy stunts—cramming and cheating in the Muggle world; eating the remains or other substances of magical creatures in the wizarding world. And wizard professors have a slightly easier task than their Muggle counterparts because they can employ anti-cheating charms. Both Muggle and wizard students receive their scores during the summer.

At the end of their education, both Muggle and wizard students take another exam: the International Baccalaureate (IB) and the N.E.W.T.s, respectively. For the IB, students are tested in six subjects (language, second language, individuals and societies, experimental sciences, mathematics, and arts) and write what's called an extended essay (4,000 words) in one subject, based on individual research that's guided by a mentor.

N.E.W.T.s, on the other hand, are Nastily Exhausting Wizarding Tests taken in the seventh (final) year at Hogwarts. Passing N.E.W.T.s is not necessary in order to graduate from Hogwarts, but good N.E.W.T. scores are required before graduates can enter certain fields. For example, to become a healer requires an "E" in N.E.W.T.s in Potions, Herbology, Transfiguration, Charms, and Defense Against the Dark Arts. And that makes sense, given that healers have to reverse the effects of potions, charms, curses, and the like. Other careers include Muggle relations, curse-breaking, professional Quidditch, retail sales, publishing, and public relations, and each has its own exam requirements.

Tourist Tip

Next time you're near a pretty, expensive boarding school, on either side of the pond, stop in and ask its motto. Chances are, it's in Latin and it waxes philosophical about the grandeur of the school and/or the students. Case in point, Eton's *Floreat Etona* ("Let Eton flourish") and Charterhouse's *Deo Dante Dedi* ("Because God has given, I give"). Hogwarts motto, on the other hand, oozes practicality: *Draco Dormiens Nunquan Titillandus* ("Never tickle a sleeping dragon").

Hagrid's Hut and the Forbidden Forest

Rebeus Hagrid, Keeper of Keys and Grounds at Hogwarts, as well as Care of Magical Creatures professor, does not live in Hogwarts castle, as do the other professors. Instead, Hagrid lives in a small hut at the edge of the grounds, near the forbidden forest, where he often ventures, in spite of the centaurs, unicorns, and giant man-eating spiders that lurk there (see Chapter 2 for more on these creatures). In the Muggle world it is not uncommon for a school's groundskeeper to live in a small building separate from—but still on the grounds of—the campus.

Just at the edge of the forbidden forest is the Whomping Willow, a tree that, when provoked (which is generally when any students are nearby), starts thrashing its long, willowy branches, breaking everything in sight. Press a knot on the tree trunk, however, and the tree ceases all movement. Fans of *The Princess Bride* movie will immediately recall the knot on the tree in that movie that reveals a secret torture chamber below.

The forest is off-limits to all students, unless they are with Hagrid or another teacher. And what would a fantasy tale be without a tempting forbidden forest? Hansel and Gretel, Sleeping Beauty, Snow White, and myriad other fairy tale characters have lost themselves in dense forests that were supposed to be off-limits. In addition, the best-known fantasy literature is teeming with dark, frightening forests: *Robin Hood's* Sherwood Forest; the dense forests of Lewis's *Narnia*; the Forest Sauvage in T.H. White's *The Once and Future King*; and the many forests in Tolkien's *The Lord of the Rings* (the Old Forest, Lothlorien, and Fanghorn Forest).

TOURIST TIP

If you're traveling to the Netherlands, put Efteling, an amusement park in the town of Kaatsheuvel, on your list for its Disney-like Fairy Tale Forest, which is comprised of authentically designed buildings nestled in a pine forest, representing scenes from ten different well-known fairy tales. Visit www.efteling.nl for details.

Hogsmeade

Hogsmeade, a village near Hogwarts, has the distinction of being the only entirely wizarding city in Great Britain. This means that, unlike Diagon Alley (see Chapter 7), which is situated in the middle of Muggle-laden London, Hogsmeade doesn't have any nonwizards nearby. Hogsmeade is a city that doesn't exist on Muggle maps, and, like Hogwarts School, it's Unplottable, so nonwizards never wander into it.

Like the school, Hogsmeade derives its name from a long connection of pigs and magic. "Mead" means both an alcoholic drink (a beverage that flows in the village pubs) and "meadow," the image of which the quaint village elicits.

And Hogsmeade is nothing if not quaint. The entire town is made up of thatched cottages and shops, just like a seventeenth-century British country town (many of which remain in the same charming state today—if you drive or take the train through the British countryside, you'll see many such quaint villages). The main street is called High Street, a name as common to British towns as "Main Street" is to small-town USA.

Hogsmeade boasts an eclectic mix of eateries and shops that rivals Diagon Alley in London. They are discussed in the remaining sections of this chapter.

Dervish and Banges

If you knew that a dervish is a whirling, chanting, frenzied person (as a part of some Muslim religious practices, not unlike the quaking and shaking that took over some Protestant groups early in U.S. history), and if you thought of the word "bang" as meaning "a loud noise," what would you think Dervish and Banges sells? If you guessed something loud and frenzied, you guessed right: Dervish and Banges sells magical wizarding instruments—which, almost by definition, because they are magical, would be unpredictable and, potentially, combustible. The actual objects sold in this store, however, are not well-documented in Rowling's novels.

Hog's Head

The Hog's Head is a pub in Hogsmeade that's not on the main road. It is, in fact, rather dark, dirty, and smelly; it's considered a far second to the Three Broomsticks (described later in this chapter), and students rarely frequent this pub. The name may be drawn from The Boar's Head in Shakespeare's *Falstaff.*

Honeydukes

A favorite of kids and adults alike, Honeydukes is a shop that sells the latest in wizard sweets, along with sweets that Muggles love, too: toffee, chocolate, and nougat (a chewy candy made from egg whites, honey, and chopped nuts).

The name likely derives from honeydew, the sweet melon, but also evokes another sweet (honey) and all things British (dukes and duchesses). There was also a Duke's Candy Store on Hoe Avenue in the Bronx in the 1960s, when J.K. Rowling was a child, but it isn't likely she ever knew it existed.

Muggles can also enjoy wizard candies without leaving the comfort of their homes. Jelly Belly sells Bertie Bott's Beans, and several online candy companies have taken to manufacturing and selling everything from Chocolate Frogs to Cockroach Clusters. See Appendix B for a few wizard candy websites.

Magic Tale

Chocolate frogs and cockroaches were first introduced to England in the 1970s in a Monty Python skit (now available on DVD) about the Whizzo Chocolate Company, which was being investigated by Inspector Praline (played by John Cleese) for using actual frogs in its Crunchy Frogs candy and real cockroaches in its Cockroach Clusters. Other candies from the skit include Ram's Bladder Cup and Anthrax Ripple.

Madam Puddifoot's Tea Shop

"Pud" is a British abbreviation for pudding, which is a creamy, mushy, often-sweet food. And creamy, mushy, and sweet is the ideal description for Madam Puddifoot's Tea Shop (which also serves coffee). Decorated with bows, lace, and other frills, the tea shop is frequented by Hogwarts couples, so there's a lot of hand-holding and smooching going on here.

Scrivenshaft's Quill Shop

Scrivenshaft's Quill Shop chose the ideal spot for a retail business that sells parchment, quills, and inks. Students burn through these supplies like water—it's the equivalent to having an Apple computer store on a college campus. Quills are not only utilitarian but also beautiful—for example, students might splurge on a long pheasant-feather quill the same way Muggle students might opt for a hot-pink iPod.

The store is aptly named: a "scrivener" is a scribe, clerk, or secretary; a "shaft" is a handle, such as that on a quill.

Three Broomsticks

The Three Broomsticks is *the* place for hot butterbeer, along with stronger beverages, such as mulled mead and red currant rum. The proprietor, Madam Rosmerta, is attractive, outgoing, and well-liked; all important attributes in a female barkeep. In Celtic mythology, Rosmerta was the goddess of abundance and good harvest.

The Three Broomsticks could also be the "inn" Hermione Granger refers to as the headquarters for the 1612 goblin rebellion, and that would give the inn a rich, interesting history.

Descriptions of the Three Broomsticks evoke a strong sense of the Shire's the Green Dragon in Tolkien's *The Lord of the Rings.* Both are described as crowded, inviting, cheerful, and smoke-filled. Of course, nearly any good bar could be described that way—and that is the point: the Three Broomsticks is a place you'd want to hang out.

Magic Tale

The magical world of Harry Potter features three pubs: the Leaky Cauldron; the Hog's Head; and the Three Broomsticks. In including pubs in her novels, Rowling follows a long tradition that began with Chaucer's *Canterbury Tales,* in which the travelers began their journey at the Tabard pub. Dickens' novels and Shakespeare's plays contain a large number of pubs (and at least in Dickens' case, he borrowed the names of real pubs); Tolkien described the Prancing Pony and the Green Dragon in *The Lord of the Rings;* and *Treasure Island* gave us the famed Admiral Benbow.

Like any thriving city, shops in Hogsmeade go out of business and/or change ownership from time to time, but the city remains a haven for wizards.

Chapter 9

International Wizarding Schools

In This Chapter

+ Finding the world's wizarding schools

+ Learning about Beauxbatons

+ Knowing more about dark Durmstrang

+ Understanding the Triwizard Tournament

Hogwarts School of Witchcraft and Wizardry isn't the only game in town; at least two other large wizarding schools exist in Europe: Beauxbatons Academy of Magic and Durmstrang Institute for Magical Study. And there are smaller schools at which you can hone your wizarding skills; but like the three largest schools, they are nearly impossible to locate without insider information, because each school guards itself and its secrets zealously.

Locating Wizarding Schools Around the World

To those who have no business being there (that is, nonmagical folks and even uninvited wizards), a wizarding school appears to be a dangerous, abandoned wreck of a building, one that would be marked "Condemned" in the Muggle world. In addition, every wizarding school is protected by spells that make it Unplottable and, thus, keep away unsuspecting Muggles and devious wizards.

KING'S ENGLISH

To **plot** is to mark the location of a building, street, or piece of land on a map. So, by definition, to **unplot** would be to remove the location of a building on a map. **Unplottable** objects take this one step further, however: they are not only removed from maps but are also removed in actual appearance. To the unaware observer, the building simply appears not to be there. Number Twelve, Grimmauld Place, the secret location of the Order of the Phoenix, is such an Unplottable building. Passersby would see Number Eleven and Number Thirteen; Number Twelve is visible only to those who have business there.

Beauxbatons Academy of Magic

Beauxbatons Academy of Magic is located in a warm, breezy palace in the Mediterranean, where students wear lightweight, luxurious silk robes. These students find Hogwarts Castle, by comparison, to be cold and damp—which, let's face it, it probably is, given the climate in Great Britain! The Beauxbatons student body is co-ed (although the girls, with their dizzying beauty, tend to take center stage), and they speak both French and thickly accented English, so we can presume the school is located in the south of France.

The coat of arms (which is more formally called a heraldic device) for the school is two crossed golden wands, each with three stars emanating from it. A wand in the magical world is akin to a sword in medieval times, and the combination of swords and stars has historically been common in heraldic devices. Finland's provinces, in particular, combine swords with stars, but so do the coats of other nations and regions. Having three stars, in particular, is common on heraldic devices of countries, states, and religious groups. In the United States, three stars on a flag or coat of arms usually refers to the three branches of government (executive, legislative, and judicial); in other parts of the world, it may relate to three provinces coming together to form a nation or to the importance of the Blessed Trinity (God, Jesus, and the Holy Spirit) in that faith. Note that, in medieval times, stars were referred to as mullets, which carried a far different meaning than that of the popular haircut of the 1980s.

Where the Name Comes From

Beaux bâtons is French for beautiful sticks, which likely refers to beautiful wands. But the girls of Beauxbatons (and their wands) are just as intelligent as they are beautiful; when they arrive at Hogwarts for a tournament, they sit at the Ravenclaw table, indicating that they are as brilliant and clever as the wizards in that Hogwarts house, which is famous for its intelligence.

TOURIST TIP

When the Beauxbatons students visit Hogwarts, a few French foods are offered for all students to try. When visiting France or the Quebec province in Canada, you can also taste the two French foods served in the Great Hall: bouillabaisse (French fish stew) and blancmange (a pink or white dessert that is rather like a thin pudding). Both have somewhat rich literary pasts: in Roman mythology, Venus used bouillabaisse to put Vulcan into a deep sleep, so that she could spend time with her other boyfriend, Mars. Blancmange has a mention in Chaucer's prologue to the *Canterbury Tales*, and is the center of one of Monty Python's more disturbing skits, in which blancmanges eat people, rather than the other way around.

A Few Key Wizards at Beauxbatons

The headmistress of Beauxbatons is Madame Olympe Maxime, who has a tanned, pleasing face but is indescribably large—clearly she has an ancestor who was a giant. However, Madame Maxime refuses to discuss this detail of her patronage because of rampant racism against wizards with giant blood somewhere in their ancestry. Hagrid, the Hogwarts groundskeeper who had a giantess mother, is smitten with Madame Maxime.

Although Madame Maxime's name could be construed to relate to her size, French for maximum is *maxima*, not *maxime*. Therefore, her name may, instead, refer to Hagrid's vision of her: *Olympe* is translated to heaven (after the God Olympus), and *maxime* is French for maxim, which is a statement of general truth; thus, "true heaven."

Fleur Delacour is Beauxbatons' most revered student; she is chosen from her school to represent Beauxbatons in the Triwizard Tournament (which is discussed later in this chapter). Fleur, like her peers, is beautiful and well-skilled in wizarding arts, but she can be less than tactful and often scorns and criticizes Hogwarts. Her first name, Fleur, is French for flower; apropos for her beauty. Her last name can be translated in a variety of ways; the most logical is beyond (*dela*) the princely court (*cour*), indicating that she is out of reach, or out of the league of, the boys at Hogwarts. She is one-quarter veela—magical creatures who seduce men with their beauty (see Chapter 2).

Durmstrang Institute for Magical Study

Whereas Beauxbatons students are beautiful, if a bit aloof, students and staff at Durmstrang are described as both unapproachable and unattractive. Although a co-ed school, boys dominate at Durmstrang, which gives every indication of being located in a cold, mountainous nation, given that students at Durmstrang wear fur capes and speak with thick Slavic accents.

The most chilling aspect of Durmstrang's curriculum is that professors teach the *use* of the Dark Arts, not just the *defense* against them, as is the practice at the other wizarding schools. Appropriately, when at Hogwarts, Durmstrang students sit at the table with Slytherin house, which has produced more Dark Wizards than any other Hogwarts house. Durmstrang's approach is roughly the equivalent to teaching students in local high schools how to make bombs: what are the odds that all students will use that information for the good of humanity? Continuing this analogy, at Hogwarts, students would learn how to diffuse bombs and how to take charge during a bomb threat!

Where the Name Comes From

Many believe Durmstrang is a wordplay on the German phrase *Strang und Durm*, which translates to "storm and stress," and that interpretation is quite likely. However, Durmstrang is probably not a German school, because the climate in Germany does not match the descriptions given by Durmstrang students. More likely, the school is located in a Slavic nation: Russia; Bulgaria; Ukraine; and the like. *Strang* translates to "strange" or "stranger" in Russian, and Durman and Durme are cities in Russia, Uzbekistan, Tajikistan, and Bosnia and Herzegovina. The name, then, might convey a sense of a strange city or strange place, rather than storm and stress, but either translation is possible.

A Few Key Wizards at Durmstrang

Head of Durmstrang was, for a number of years, Professor Igor Karkaroff, a former Death Eater (that is, a follower of Lord Voldemort; see Chapter 1). Igor is a common name in Slavic countries, and stories such as *The Winter of Prince Igor* and *The Song of Igor's Campaign* flourish in Russian literature. Karkaroff is a common Bulgarian surname.

Viktor Krum, an 18-year-old student at Durmstrang, is the school's most well-known student. A world-renowned Quidditch Seeker, Krum's athletic accomplishments make girls swoon. Viktor is a familiar Slavic name for boys and also means "victor"; appropriate for the best Seeker in the world. Krum's last name is just as filled with promise: Krum was the name of a ninth century ruler (also called a khan or tsar) of Bulgaria who was among that country's most influential leaders, expanding the borders of his country, nearly conquering Constantinople, and establishing a written rule of law. For a young Bulgarian hero to have the name Krum is like a young American hero being called Washington.

Interschool Rivalry: The Triwizard Tournament

From roughly 1300 to 1900, the three largest wizarding schools in Europe came together every five years to compete in the Triwizard Tournament, a test of wizarding skills among three contestants—one from each school—who competed not only for a cash prize but also for personal and school glory. Each school rotated its turn as host, with the other two schools sending a small group of potential contestants to live at the school for that year. The contest—discontinued for more than 100 years after a number of students died—was recently revived and held at Hogwarts.

Choosing *three* schools for the competition is probably more about keeping the competition manageable than anything else. All three schools are roughly the same size, thus eliminating the complaints about large schools competing with smaller ones that plague many state-wide high-school sporting contests in the United States. And two contingents of guests from visiting schools is a manageable amount to house for nearly an entire school year. Had five, eight, or more schools been involved in a Pentawizard or Octowizard Tournament, the result may have been more chaotic. In addition, including three schools continues a long tradition in magical and fairy realms. The number three is (along with the number seven) one of two oft-used numbers in mythology and fairy tales: think of Goldilocks and her three bears, the three pigs, and three billy goats gruff, along with the many stories of three sons, the youngest of whom succeeds when his older siblings fail at a task.

Interschool competition exists throughout the nonwizarding community in Europe, including sports competitions (in soccer, cricket, and rugby) and academically oriented competitions like problem-solving, mathematics, science competition, web design, linguistics, and so on. Although these contests rarely last for an entire year, schoolchildren do travel from country to country to compete, much like some national-caliber U.S. high school teams travel several hundred miles to compete in high-level competitions.

Part 4

Spells, Potions, and Other Ways of Performing Magic

In this part, you get to read the detailed backstory on how J.K. Rowling chose the names and functions of dozens of wizard herbs, potions, and spells. You also get detailed information on some of the special, high-level spells and tools that only a select few wizards will ever use.

Chapter 10

Herbology 101

In This Chapter

+ Discovering the history of many common herbs

+ Recognizing that most wizard plants exist in the natural world

+ Understanding the most common wizarding plants

Herbology is the study of plants and is taught at all good wizarding schools. Herbs have, in fact, been a key component of a healer's toolbox for millennia, dating back beyond ancient Greece and Rome. Many of today's Muggle pharmaceuticals still use herbs and plants as their base.

This chapter gives you an overview of the primary herbs and plants that exist in the wizarding world. First you'll find out what we know about each plant or herb in the nonwizarding world, including its botanical name, characteristics, and medicinal uses (if any). That's followed by a brief look at how each herb or plant is used in the wizarding world. For plants that exist only in the wizarding world, as is the case with those at the end of this chapter, you'll get a behind-the-scenes look at why

Rowling may have chosen each particular plant's name and characteristics. (Be sure to also check out Chapter 11 for in-depth information on magical potions.)

The Link Between Herbs and Magical Potions

Witches have long been rumored to use herbs to make potions, and in Rowling's wizarding world, herbs have that vital function. Many herbs, along with eyeballs, livers, and the like from a variety of creatures—plus the occasional magical stone—make up the essential elements of potions, which are used both to cast spells and to cure everything from acne to broken bones.

On the other hand, some herbs and plants are not used in potions but are interesting in and of themselves. Like Muggles, some wizards have a green thumb and simply like to surround themselves with interesting plants. And if you thought the Venus Flytrap was "interesting," wait until you see some of the wizard plants in this chapter!

Magic Tale

You can find herbs in everything from Greek literature to twentieth-century fantasy novels:

+ Odysseus (in Homer's *Odyssey*) uses moly to protect him from Circe's spells.

+ Aragorn (in Tolkien's *The Fellowship of the Ring*) uses the herb athelas to help Frodo survive the wound inflicted by the Black Riders.

+ In Le Guin's *The Wizard of Earthsea*, Ged learns the names and uses of all the herbs in the land.

+ Even in C.S. Lewis's *The Lion, the Witch and the Wardrobe*, Lucy receives a gift from Father Christmas of a cordial of healing potion—we can assume it contains an herb of some sort.

Plants and Herbs You Know and Love

The plants and herbs in this section exist in the Muggle world—in fact, you could buy any of these plants and grow them in your garden. You may not have the wizarding skills to boil them up into potent potions, but you'd have the raw ingredients.

Aconite

Aconite is from the *Aconitum* genus of the buttercup family, and is considered highly poisonous. Tiny amounts can slow down the heart and lungs for medical purposes, but larger amounts are toxic. It is also known by two other words: monkshood and wolfsbane.

+ *Monkshood:* The terms monkshood (monks + hood) comes from the shape of the flower, which looks (as you may have guessed) like the hood of a monk's cloak.

+ *Wolfsbane:* The term wolfsbane comes from its use by Greeks as a way to poison wolves; "bane" means to kill. (See Chapter 11 for more on Wolfsbane Potion.)

In the wizarding world, aconite is used in a variety of potions.

> ## Magic Tale
>
> Near the end of C.S. Lewis's *The Lion, the Witch and the Wardrobe,* when Peter kills Fenris Ulf, Aslan knights Peter, calling him "Sir Peter Wolfs-Bane" ("Sir Peter Fenris-Bane" in some editions; "fenris" means "wolf"), because he killed such a terrible and mighty wolf.

Asphodel

Asphodel is a member of the *Ashodeline* genus of the lily family. It looks like a lily, with white or yellow flowers and narrow green leaves.

Asphodel has long been known as the flower of death; in fact, it is thought to be the flower that the dead like the most! For this reason, asphodel used to be planted in and around tombs.

In the wizarding world, asphodel is used in the Draught of Living Death.

Belladonna

Belladonna *(Atropa belladonna)* goes by several names, most of which have "deadly" or "devil" in the title. It is a highly poisonous plant of the nightshade family (which also includes tobacco, red peppers, tomatoes, potatoes, eggplant, and petunias), with purple or red flowers and black berries.

The *Atropa* portion of its botanical name is derived from Atropos, one of the Greek Fates. The *belladonna* portion is translated as "beautiful woman." Confused? Venetian women once used belladonna to dilate their pupils, which was supposed to make them more beautiful. We can be grateful that some of history's great beauty secrets lasted only a generation or two.

Long used as a way to poison unsuspecting rivals, in tiny amounts it has also been used to combat migraines, lower heart rate, and relax bronchial and urinary muscles.

Belladonna is used so often in wizarding potions that it is part of the potion-making kit purchased by all Hogwarts Potions students.

Daisy

The daisy *(Chrysanthemum leucanthemum)* is so common, with its white flowers and yellow center, that it is sometimes considered a weed among Muggles. Daisy roots, however, are used in the wizarding world to make a Shrinking Solution, which makes some sense, because an old wives' tale says that daisy roots, boiled in milk and fed to a farm animal, can stop the animal from growing too large.

Fluxweed

Fluxweed *(Isanthus brachiatus)* is also called false pennyroyal and is a member of the mint family.

A key ingredient in wizard Polyjuice Potion (which makes one wizard look like another for a brief period of time), fluxweed is commonly used in the wizarding world. To be useful in that particular potion, however, the fluxweed must be harvested during a full moon.

Note that "flux," from the Latin *fluxus,* means flow. In electronics design and manufacturing, flux is a product that makes solder flow better across circuit boards. In physics, flux is the rate of flow of energy across a surface. In the movie *Back to the Future,* Doc Brown tells Marty that his flux capacitor makes time travel possible.

Ginger

Ginger *(Zingiber officinale)* is an herb that's used both as a spice and as a medicinal plant. It is known to calm the digestive system, which is why ginger tea and ginger ale are given to people with upset stomachs.

In the wizarding world, ginger must have an effect on the brain as well; wizards use ginger roots to make a Wit-Sharpening Potion.

TOURIST TIP

Ginger is an effective deterrent against motion sickness. If you have a tendency to get car- or airsick, take a thermos of ginger tea with you and sip it as you travel. (If the airline won't let you take a thermos, bring along a few ginger tea bags.) Look for ginger tea in supermarkets and health-food stores.

Hellebore

Hellebore—also called Christherb because it flowers near Christmas—is unusual in that it is from both the *Helleborus* genus of the buttercup family (as is aconite) and the *Veratrum* genus of the lily family (as is asphodel). It's highly poisonous, either killing or causing severe burning to the skin if handled and to the intestines if ingested. Tiny amounts, however, can stimulate the heart, and people have historically blessed their farm animals with hellebore.

The name is said to originate from the Greek for "plant eaten by fawns." Apparently, it's not poisonous to deer. It may also come from the Greek *elein*, meaning "to injure," and *bora*, meaning food—injurious food, which makes sense given how poisonous the substance is.

In the wizarding world, the syrup from the hellebore plant is used in the Draught of Peace.

Knotgrass

Knotgrass is from the *Polygonum* genus of the buckwheat family and is a common weed or grass with thin stems and leaves and small flowers. Like daisy roots boiled in milk, knotgrass is thought to limit the growth of animals. Shakespeare mentions knotgrass in *A Midsummer Night's Dream*.

In the wizarding world, knotgrass is used in Polyjuice Potion and is likely how the potion gets its name (from the botanical name *Polygonum*).

Lovage

This plant (botanical name, *Levisticum officianle*) is a member of the umbel family (which is in the same family as celery and parsley). It has long been a home remedy, often in the form of a medicinal tea.

In the wizarding world, lovage is used to make a Confusing and Befuddlement Draught.

Mallowsweet

The mallow is a family of plants with large flowers that bloom on a large stalk or tube; hollyhock is a good example. Mallowsweet is not a recognized variety in the Muggle world, but would likely come from that same family, perhaps as a sweet-tasting variety. In the wizarding world, centaurs burn mallowsweet and sage, and receive divine wisdom from the shapes of the flames and smoke.

Mandrake

The mandrake (*Mandragora officinarum*) is a member of the nightshade family; a small, round, purple plant that's essential to potion-making, especially antidotes. This plant has historically been thought to have magical qualities, because its roots look somewhat human-like.

In the wizarding world, one of its properties is that it can return a person to his or her human state—if a curse or transfiguration-gone-wrong has trapped the person in a nonhuman body or if the person has been petrified. Wear earplugs or earmuffs, however, when repotting mandrakes (which must be done three times in the first nine months), because the "root" of a mandrake looks like a tiny baby and, when the plant is fully grown, the root makes a wailing cry that is fatal to the listener.

Nettle

Nettle is from the *Urtica* genus of the nettle family, and is a stingy, spiny, thorny plant. The plant is so bothersome that the word "nettle" has come to mean "to irritate." Nettle is, however, used in teas and soups to help with digestive disorders.

One of the most interesting mentions of nettle in Biblical times was in the Old Testament during the calamity of Job (pronounced johb). During this dismal time in Job's life, his opponents hid behind nettles, and the thorns served as protection for them, rather than harming them. Poor Job. Nothing ever seemed to go his way.

In the wizarding world, nettle is used as a cure for boils. But this isn't so unusual. In the Muggle world, especially in Britain, drinking nettle tea is used as a treatment for boils. The herb called blind nettle (which is actually a mint, not a nettle) has also traditionally been used to treat boils.

Pomegranate

Pomegranate (*Punica granatum*) is a bright-red fruit borne on a small tree. Inside, the fruit is full of seeds from which pomegranate juice is made. The juice is prized for its high potassium content, which makes pure pomegranate juice expensive when compared to other fruit juices. The fruit was historically used as a red dye and in tanning leather, has been used medicinally, and is a symbol of fertility. In the Bible, Solomon's temple contained many pomegranate carvings.

Pomegranate juice is used in the wizarding world, but be careful when making a Strengthening Solution, because your bottle of pomegranate juice may be carelessly mistaken for the correct ingredient, salamander blood.

Sage

Sage is from the *Salvia* genus of the mint family that is used for decoration and for seasoning foods, especially chicken, meats, cheeses, and so on. It is derived from the Latin *salvus*, which means "safe."

"Safe" sage has many healing powers. Most recently, sage has been shown to help asthmatics, who breathe it in during attacks.

In the wizarding world, centaurs mix sage with mallowsweet in divination.

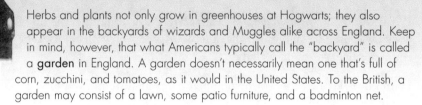

KING'S ENGLISH

Herbs and plants not only grow in greenhouses at Hogwarts; they also appear in the backyards of wizards and Muggles alike across England. Keep in mind, however, that what Americans typically call the "backyard" is called a **garden** in England. A garden doesn't necessarily mean one that's full of corn, zucchini, and tomatoes, as it would in the United States. To the British, a garden may consist of a lawn, some patio furniture, and a badminton net.

Scurvy-grass

Scurvy-grass (*Cochlearia officianlis;* also called scurvy weed) is a northern plant from the crucifer family that was traditionally used to treat scurvy, a disease caused by a deficiency of Vitamin C and resulting in anemia, weak bones, and other nasty symptoms. Scurvy was common among those traveling long distances by ship, when no fresh fruits and vegetables were available. Today, with the advent of vitamins, scurvy has mostly disappeared. However, describing scurvy is still how fifth-grade teachers get you to eat oranges and grapefruit.

In the wizarding world, scurvy-grass is used to make Confusing and Befuddlement Draughts.

Sneezewort

Sneezewort is a kind of yarrow (*Achillea ptarmica*), which causes sneezing in many people. (Can you say, highly allergenic?) Keep in mind that "wort" simply means "plant" or "herb," so a sneezewort is a plant that relates to sneezing.

Sneezewort, along with lovage and scurvy-grass, is used in the wizarding world to make Confusing and Befuddlement Draughts.

Valerian

Valerian (*Aleriana officinalis*) is derived from the Latin *valere*, meaning "to be healthy." It is also known as garden heliptrope and tobacco root and has for centuries been used as a sleep aid. In fact, valerian tablets and teas are commonly sold as an herbal remedy for inducing sleep.

In the wizarding world, valerian is used in the Draught of Living Death, which is appropriate, given valerian's well-known soporific qualities.

Wormwood

Wormwood (*Artemisia judaica*) is a shrub in the aster family, the oil of which was used to make absinthe, a liqueur that is now illegal in some countries because of its toxicity.

Found in Palestine, the wormwood plant appears often in the Bible, serving as a metaphor for sadness in several portions of the Old Testament. The New Testament references the plant in conjunction with God's punishment of the Israelites.

In the wizarding world, wormwood is used in the Draught of Living Death, perhaps because although it is lethal in large quantities, it can be taken in small amounts.

Wormwood is also the name of the junior tempter in C.S. Lewis's *The Screwtape Letters*. In the book, Wormwood's Uncle Screwtape writes him a series of letters, in which he attempts to teach Wormwood how to become a professional devil, winning human hearts to "Our Father Below." The name is meant to convey a disgusting, belly-crawling creature.

Wizard-Only Plants and Herbs

A few plants and herbs grow only in the wizarding world—no such varieties exist in Muggle gardens, plant stores, or herb shops. The following sections shed light on this unusual wizard-only vegetation.

Abyssinian Shrivelfigs

Abyssinian Shrivelfigs grow as a stalk that must be pruned from time to time. The figs themselves are skinned and used in a Shrinking Solution.

Figs are, however, historically significant. Greek goddess Demeter was supposed to have introduced figs to humans (on the Roman side, the god Bacchus is given responsibility for the introduction of the fig), and the Greeks continued to think highly of this fruit—it was the primary training food of the first Olympians. After all, who needs meat and potatoes when you have figs?

Homer's *Iliad* and *Odyssey* both mention figs. Figs are also the most oft-mentioned fruit in the Bible. Recently, anthropologists discovered that figs are the oldest cultivated crop known to man, when several petrified figs were found in the Jordan Valley and evaluated for their age.

Abyssinia is an older name for the country of Ethiopia but, ironically, Ethiopia's main crops are coffee and grains, not figs. (Most of the world's figs are grown in California and the Mediterranean.) And figs are a shrively sort of fruit, at least when they're dried—dried figs are the most common form. Their shriveled skin actually looks a bit like a walnut's shell, except that a fig is soft to the touch, not hard like a walnut.

Today, figs are enjoyed primarily in gourmet recipes and, of course, in Fig Newtons.

Bubotubers

This plant looks like a large slug with boils on it, which are filled with pus. The boils can be squeezed and the pus collected; when diluted, it's used to treat severe acne. Undiluted, however, it can damage the skin, so when squeezing the boils, wizards wear dragon-skin gloves.

Tuber is Latin for tumor, which makes sense. But *bubo* is Latin for horned owl, and that's where we lose any probable translation, as the plant hardly resembles a tumor-filled horned owl.

Devil's Snare

Devil's Snare looks like several large snakes: the plant has huge tendrils that twist around your limbs and squeeze you to death. It dies in daylight, in dry conditions, and when exposed to fire. Devil's snare is very much like the creature that attacked Frodo (in *The Fellowship of the Ring*) at the passageway inside Moria; what Tolkien described as "a host of snakes" that were trying to wrap their way around Frodo and strangle him.

One can also think of Devil's Snare like the Southern weed kudzu, which grows rampantly and multiplies so quickly that it squeezes out every other plant in its path.

Gillyweed

Gillyweed is another unattractive plant: it grows in long, green-gray, spaghetti-like tendrils about a quarter-inch in diameter. Gillyweed (translating loosely to "a weed that gives you gills") sets you up for underwater travel: ingesting the plant allows you, for one hour, to breathe and swim like an amphibian. You sprout gills, grow webs between your fingers and toes, and can withstand the cold temperature of water.

Gillyweed is, essentially, the wizard equivalent of Scuba equipment (which lets you breathe underwater) and a wet suit (which allows your body to withstand cold underwater temperature). Just think of all the money wizards save on Scuba gear rental!

Sopophorous Bean

Sopophorous bean is used in the Draught of Living Death. The word "soporific" is an SAT word that means "causing sleep"; it's from the Latin *spoor*, meaning sleep. This makes sense, given that living death is a comalike state—a deep sleep.

Venomous Tentacula

This red plant has long feelers that seize you from behind when you're least expecting it. You can, however, slap it away if you notice the feelers encircling you. The black, shriveled seeds (which are of unknown use) are a Class C Non-Tradeable Substance, which means if you try to sell them, you'd get in big trouble with the Ministry, buster.

Tentacula is likely a play on "tentacle" and "Dracula," the blood-sucking vampire. That the plant is red is an interesting twist on the healing powers of plants. Traditionally, any red plant was useful in *treating* "red" medical problems—that is, blood disorders, bloody injuries, and the like. But this particular red plant is itself out for blood, so to speak.

Chapter 11

Round About the Cauldron Go: Draughts and Potions

In This Chapter

+ Gathering potion-making tools

+ Getting the lowdown on insects and creatures

+ Finding a list of common magical potions

Magical potions—what we might think of as "witch's brew"—give wizards the power to heal, kill, extract the truth, and produce a variety of other behaviors and emotions. Potions are produced in cauldrons, using mostly herbs and portions of insects or other creatures. This chapter shares the secrets of the most well-known potions, as well as some of the key ingredients that go into them.

One more note before moving on to the ins and outs of potions: one of the reference books mentioned in Rowling's novels is *Moste Potente Potions*, a book whose name is not meant to be difficult to pronounce, but instead recalls Middle English, spoken in the British Isles from 1066 c.e. to about 1550.

KING'S ENGLISH

The English language can be divided into three periods: Old English (approximately 450 c.e.–1066 c.e., a blend of Celtic and Old Norse languages; Middle English (1066–1550), with a strong Latin and French influence; and Modern English (1550–present). Although Old English is unreadable to an English speaker, Middle English can be understood, but reading it is slow going. For example, from Chaucer's Tale of Melibeus: "and the moste parte of that companye have scorned these olde wise men." Basically, to master Middle English, you talk with a lot of pomp and fluff, and you add an "e" to the end of moste

Basic Tools: Cauldrons, Flagons, Phials, and Scales

Wizards—both those who are in training and those with experience—primarily use four tools to make potions:

+ A *cauldron* (also spelled "caldron") is a large metal pot used to boil liquids (or, for that matter, to make Muggle stew or chili). It may be made of copper, brass, pewter, or silver, and, if charmed correctly, may be collapsible (easier for carrying) or self-stirring (no bits of lacewings burning to the bottom of the cauldron). For a brief history of cauldrons, see the "Cauldron Shop" section in Chapter 7.

+ Better known as a flask, a *flagon* is a container or bottle for beverages (usually alcoholic ones, in the Muggle world) that has a short or narrow neck and may have a handle, spout, or lid. A flagon also refers to what's inside the bottle, so a "flagon of whiskey" is an actual amount, akin to a "pint of whiskey." Rowling doesn't discuss the actual uses of flagons in the wizarding world, but presumably, they hold ingredients for potions.

+   From the Latin *phialia* and the Greek *phiale*, *phial* is also *vial* in English: a small glass bottle, often used for storing medicines. Phials are used for storing prepared potions by inserting a stopper in the top of the bottle, sealing the contents for future use.

+   A *scale* is another word for a weighing balance, which was an old way to weigh objects. It works a bit like a seesaw. Place an object of known mass (say, one ounce) on one side of the scale, and another object of unknown mass on the other side of the scale. If the scale tips to the side of the unknown object, it weighs more than one ounce; if it tips to the side of the known object, the unknown object weighs less than one ounce. (Potions sometimes require precise amounts of ingredients, which would need to be of a certain weight or volume, as is the case when Muggles bake and need to get the exact amount of flour into the cake. On the other hand, as is the case with other types of Muggle cooking, potions sometimes require only "close-enough" amounts, like a pinch of rat's tail.)

In addition, knives and other cutting instruments are used to chop, grind, and grate ingredients.

The herbs and insects/creatures that go into most potions can be found in an apothecary (see Chapter 7). The ingredients can also be grown or collected on your own, but buying them is certainly cleaner and easier. Ingredients can be bought individually or as part of potion-making kits.

Magic Tale

Besides Rowling's novels, perhaps the best-known literary work depicting cauldrons is Shakespeare's Scottish play, *Macbeth*. In Act IV, Scene I, witches throw into a cauldron ingredients that surely influenced Rowling: snake fillet, newt eye, frog toe, dog tongue, owl wing, lizard leg, dragon scale, wolf tooth, baboon blood, and so on! As these ingredients are tossed into a cauldron, three witches incant, "Double, double toil and trouble; fire burn, and cauldron bubble."

Insects and Other Creatures

In the magical world, an unusual assortment of insects and parts of other creatures finds their way into potions, including the following slimy, scaly, slippery stuff (see Chapter 2 for more details on many of these creatures):

+ *Scarab beetles:* Used mashed-up or powdered, scarab beetles were considered sacred in ancient Egypt, where the beetles' form was used on amulets. Also called a dung beetle because of what it feeds on. See the "Wit-Sharpening Potion" section later in this chapter for more on scarab beetles and the Egyptians.

+ *Powdered horn of bicorn:* The bicorn is a fabled beast, the gender equivalent of a chichevache: legend had long held that the chichevache feeds exclusively on "good women" and is, therefore, thin and meager-looking, because its food source is so scarce. (You see where this is going?) The bicorn, on the other hand, feeds only on "good and enduring husbands," and is, therefore, nice and plump from all its available food source! Hmmm.

+ *Shredded boomslang skin:* A boomslang is a large, highly poisonous African snake that's also called the tree snake. Its shredded skin is used in Polyjuice Potion.

+ *Caterpillar:* Caterpillars (the larval stage of butterflies and moths) are not generally seen as magical creatures; however, Rowling's mention of caterpillars in potions may be a nod to Lewis Carroll's giant caterpillar in *Alice's Adventures in Wonderland.* Caterpillars do end up in the Shrinking Solution (discussed later in this chapter), which also calls Alice to mind.

+ *Cockroach:* I say, "good riddance." Who could have a problem losing a few of the world's cockroaches to a bubbling cauldron? On the other hand, keep in mind that potions often have to be ingested to work their magic, so maybe cockroaches aren't so tenable.

+ *Crocodile heart:* In the Old Testament, a crocodile is seen in the same vein as a serpent (or snake), so think of a crocodile like a snake, which is a highly prized magical creature.

+ *Lacewing flies:* Also called lacewings, this beneficial insect has gauzy wings and voraciously eats aphids for dinner. Also called golden-eye flies and stink flies because of their odor.

+ *Leeches and leech juice:* A leech is a worm that sucks on flesh and blood; leeches have a long (if dubious) medicinal history, so their inclusion in potions is to be expected.

+ *Porcupine quills:* Native Americans, especially the Lakota, have long used porcupine quills in decoration and consider the porcupine to have magical qualities.

+ *Puffer-fish eyes:* The puffer-fish (also spelled pufferfish and puffer fish) is also called blowfish and bubblefish, because it can blow up its body—and, thus, appear much larger—when threatened. Puffer-fish eyes are known in the Muggle world to be highly toxic.

+ *Rat spleen and pickled rats' brains:* Rats are an important animal in the wizarding world because they are often kept as pets. It is, then, a bit surprising that rat parts are used in potions!

+ *Salamander blood:* Salamanders have a long association with dragons (given that they look like tiny dragons themselves). Salamander blood is used in a Strengthening Solution. Shelled salamander eggs can also be used to feed magical creatures.

+ *Stewed horned slugs:* Although "horned slugs" is not an official term used in the Muggle world, slugs do look like they have small horns, so the term does not likely refer to a magical creature but to the lowly garden slug. And what better way to get rid of them than to add them to your favorite magical brew?

+ *Crushed snake fangs:* Snake fangs would be difficult to procure, unless the snake were already dead. But snakes and serpents are among the most magical of all creatures, so it makes sense that snake fangs would be highly prized for their magical qualities.

+ *Unicorn horn and tail:* The highly magical horn and tail of this magical creature are occasionally used in potions, because removing either a horn or tail from a unicorn will not kill it. The blood of a unicorn, on the other hand, is never used in potions. Unicorn blood has great power, in that it will keep you alive even if you are seconds from death, but you will lead a cursed life from that moment on.

Common Draughts, Potions, and Antidotes

The final section of this chapter lists the common potions you'll find in the wizarding world, most of which clean something, cure some ailment, or cause wizards to behave in ways they otherwise wouldn't. Each of the following sections describes the purpose of the potion, lists its ingredients (if known), and discusses any additional mythological, Biblical, or literary background.

KING'S ENGLISH

Draught is a British way to spell "draft," but both are pronounced the same way. From the Middle English word for drawing or pulling (like pulling an oar), the word has numerous meanings. But in the magical world, a draught is a drink or potion (most likely, a nasty-tasting one) that treats or prevents some terrible malady.

Aging Potion

Muggles spend billions of dollars on creams, injections, and surgery to make a person appear younger. Even in fairy tales, witches and hags make themselves appear much younger (and beautiful), but never intentionally age themselves. So fixated are we, in fact, on making ourselves younger and in promoting youth that the term "ageism" was coined in the late 1960s, and has now come into common usage in the English language: an action indicating or portrayal that assumes a person is lesser because of age.

Yet this wizarding potion does the opposite, temporarily aging the potion drinker, either ever-so-slightly (say, by a few weeks or months) or a great deal (years or decades). An Age Line spell, however, can block an Aging Potion, so that no one is fooled by the new, older age.

This potion would get a lot of mileage in the Muggle world among 8-year-olds who really want to go on that roller-coaster ride and 20-year-olds who really want to go into that bar. Of course, one would expect powerful anti-aging spells (including the Age Line spell) at both types of locations.

Amortentia

From the Latin *amor* (love) and *tentamen* (attempt or effort), Amortentia is a powerful love potion, one that's described as "most dangerous and powerful." The potion doesn't actually create love, but instead causes the taker to be strongly attracted to, and perhaps even obsessed with, a particular witch or wizard. Both Muggles and wizards can fall under the spell of Amortentia.

The danger of all love potions is that they eventually wear off, leaving the affected person no longer moony over his or her love object—much like a crush in the Muggle world. And even while the potion is in effect, the couple is not really in a relationship, because the one affected by Amortentia is completely befuddled by his or her infatuation. This potion, then, creates more of a temporary crush or infatuation than anything resembling true love. Not even wizards can create that!

Babbling Beverage

This potion causes someone to babble nonsensically. Its ingredients—and, admittedly, its purpose—are a mystery. However, the opposite potion, a non-Babbling Beverage, would be mighty popular among people with verbose spouses/girlfriends/boyfriends and among exhausted parents of toddlers and tweens.

The word "babble" is found in a number of languages, including Latin (*balbulus*), Dutch (*babbelen*), Icelandic (*babbla*), and Sanskrit (*balbala-kr*). Because the word is associated with the sounds babies make before they learn to talk, babies likely make those same sounds (that is, "ba, ba, ba") in all cultures; hence the same word is used the world over.

Blood-Replenishing Potion

This potion acts like a blood transfusion, putting lost blood back into the body. The ingredients are unknown, but leeches—which are known for the opposite quality, called *bloodletting*—are probably not on the ingredients list.

Bloodletting, through the use of leeches, was a medical practice started by Ancient Egyptians and continued as late as the 1960s. Leeches were placed strategically on a patient's body and allowed to feed on the patient's blood until satiated—roughly a half hour. Recently, the practice has been revived to help patients who have insufficient blood drainage following surgeries. The leeches' saliva produces an anti-clotting compound, a local anesthetic, and a good bacterium that kills harmful bacteria. University of Wisconsin scientists have even recently invented a synthetic leech.

Bulbadox Powder

Bulbadox Powder is one of those really awful potions that can be used only to wreak havoc on the unsuspecting user—it causes boils, which are large, painful infections on the skin. The name is likely derived from the word "bulbaceous" (a synonym for "bulbous"), which means bulb-shape (as, unfortunately, a raging boil is!). The ingredients of Bulbadox Powder are unknown, but a potion to cure boils contains nettles (see Chapter 10), snake fangs, stewed horned slugs, and porcupine quills. Stinging nettles, porcupine quills, and snake fangs are not the sort of soothing, calming ingredients you might expect to see in an anti-boil potion, but nettle tea has long been used as a treatment for boils, especially in Great Britain.

Confusing and Befuddlement Draught (also Confusing Concoction)

A Confusing and Befuddlement Draught is meant to befuddle and, therefore, distract the user. This potion is likely used on Muggles who have seen possible wizard activities, but think of how a rather evil wizard could find it useful in other situations: pouring a smidgeon into his dad's nightcap just before he checks the clock to see how late he got home; sharing a little with a police officer as he or she is writing him a ticket or to a bank teller or store clerk who is counting out his change; slipping a little to a witnesses in a court case. A good wizard could easily go bad with powers such as these.

Confusing potions aren't unique to the wizarding world. George Eliot wrote about a "confusing potion" in her 1876 novel, *Daniel Deronda* (her last). Long before that, Sophocles wrote that Athena tricked Ajax into confusing sheep with men—which is highly inconvenient during war-time! Key ingredients include lovage (historically used as a medicinal tea), scurvy-grass (once a treatment for scurvy or vitamin C deficiency), and sneezewort (a form of yarrow to which many people are allergic). See Chapter 10 for more on these ingredients, all of which you can grow in your backyard.

Doxycide

Forget what you know (or can look up) about the word "doxy." This potion is *not* intended to get rid of women of ill repute (a "doxy") as the name might suggest; in the wizarding world, a doxy is an evil, fairy-like animal with four arms, four legs, sharp teeth, and wings. Doxycide, derived from the word "doxy" and the suffix –cide, which means "to kill" (as in the word "pesticide"), is a black liquid that paralyzes doxies with just one squirt. Its ingredients are unknown.

Dr. Ubbly's Oblivious Unction

To be "oblivious" is to be unaware, and "unction" refers to an oil or salve, usually a soothing or comforting one, used for religious or medicinal purposes. ("Unction" also refers to rubbing into or sprinkling oil onto the body; thus, Extreme Unction is the term used by the Catholic Church for the Anointing of the Sick, also called Last Rites.) Because we don't know the ingredients for this potion, nor do we know anything about Dr. Ubbly, we can only assume that it is a salve of some sort that's intended to make people oblivious to the world around them (and could, therefore, have a strong connection to—or even be the same potion as—a Confusing Concoction) or forget something uncomfortable or terrifying they've seen.

One note, however: doctors don't exist in the wizarding world, so this potion may have originated in the Muggle world. "Healer Ubbly" would be more likely, if this were, indeed, a uniquely wizard potion. Ubbly, on the other hand, evokes a strong sense of a bubbling cauldron (ubbly-bubbly).

Draught of Living Death

The Draught of Living Death is a sleep potion unlike any other—it produces a sleep so powerful that it mimics death. Could this be what Sleeping Beauty was given? Or Juliet?

This complicated potion—which starts off as a black-colored potion and eventually changes to a pale pink—contains all the best sleep aids.

✦ *Valarian:* This herb has long be used in Muggle teas as a sleep aid.

✦ *Sopophorous bean:* "Soporific" means "causing sleep."

✦ *Asphodel:* Known as the "flower of death," people plant this around gravestones to honor the dead.

✦ *Wormwood:* This plant with toxic qualities is used poetically as a metaphor for sadness.

The Draught of Living Death may be the same potion as one mentioned in the wizarding world (but never named) that is supposed to cause dreamless sleep.

Draught of Peace

Possibly the same as a Calming Draught, the Draught of Peace calms anxiety, irritation, frustration, and agitation. In other words, it makes you chill. Excellent, dude.

The only known ingredients are syrup from the hellebore plant (which is highly poisonous but has been used medicinally in small quantities) and powdered moonstone (which is a stone of unknown origin). Other ingredients are likely similar to those of the Draught of Living Death, albeit in far smaller quantities.

Hellebore has been known for at least a century as a powerful physical depressant, lowering pulse rate and even creating a light form of paralysis in patients. With too high a dose, patients can die from asphyxia, but at the proper dosage, hellebore begins to immediately calm patients.

Elixir of Life

In the Muggle world, an *elixir* is a sweet solution in which the sometimes-nasty taste of drugs is hidden—a spoonful of sugar helping the medicine go down, so to speak.

But the Elixir of Life, in both the Muggle and wizarding worlds, is something altogether different. For millennia, alchemists (half scientists, half magicians) searched for this elusive elixir, which is produced from the equally elusive Philosopher's Stone (and called about a thousand other names), which is said to bring immortality to the drinker. Although no one was ever proven to have discovered this potion, alchemists in many parts of the world, over the course of hundreds of years, tried valiantly. Alchemy was, for a long time, considered a noble profession, one that usually involved an apprenticeship with a master alchemist. A second primary goal of alchemists, along with finding this fountain of youth, was to find a process for turning base metals into gold.

One man is repeatedly mentioned as having succeeded in his quest for the Elixir of Life: Nicolas Flamel, who allegedly drank the potion and shared it with his wife, Pernelle. Only one sticking point here: Flamel lived to be about 70. Granted, 70 was pretty old in the fourteenth and fifteenth centuries, but still, one would think the Elixir of Life would create immortality longer than 70 years. (For more on Flamel, see Chapter 1.)

Suffice it to say that, for thousands of years, people have been searching for a way to stay young and be rich. Alchemists are no different.

Elixir to Induce Euphoria

Euphoria is a feeling of great joy or excitement, and this potion produces those feelings in someone who is less than excited. Its ingredients are unknown, but we can guess at them, based on Muggle versions of feel-good tea, which include everything from rooibos, an African plant made into teas, to brandy and cognac, which have obvious euphoric qualities.

Eastern teas that are meant to induce euphoria include the following ingredients: gota kula (known to stimulate a startle response in the brain); yerba mate (which contains stimulants that are in the same family as those in coffee and cocoa); and damiana (a plant with leaves that, when smoked, produce a relaxing effect).

> ### Magic Tale
>
> The Elixir to Induce Euphoria has been known to, among other things, lead to "excessive ... nose-tweaking." Similarly, in the Disney version of *Mary Poppins*, Dick Van Dyke sings about getting his nose tweaked until he learned the magic word. But just what *is* nose-tweaking? It's a sharp pinch or twist of the nose, meant to be a prank or joke. Oh, yeah. That sounds *really* fun, doesn't it?

"Euphoria" is also the name of a line of juice bars that serve energizing smoothies and teas throughout the UK. The company's motto is "Positive Thinking. Positive Drinking."

Felix Felicis

Felix Felicis is liquid luck, creating situations in which everything goes your way. *Felix* and *felicis* both are the same word in Latin, meaning fruitful, lucky, happy, fortunate, and successful. In other words, Felix Felicis is bottled confidence.

For obvious reasons, Felix Felicis is banned in the competitive arena (sports, exams, elections, and so on), but what's interesting about this potion is that the *belief* that one has taken it can be as powerful as actually consuming the potion. But that is true in the Muggle world as well: if one firmly believes in his ability to accomplish something, it is far more likely to be accomplished than if he doesn't believe in it.

Magic Tale

Felix the Cat was a movie cartoon from the early twentieth-century silent film era that was revived as a TV cartoon in the 1950s. In the TV version, Felix had a Magic Bag of Tricks, which were shapeshifters that Felix could control and that could get him out of any mess. This sly, grinning, confident cat acted, in fact, just like a wizard on a dose of Felix Felicis.

Hiccupping Solution

Does a Hiccupping Solution cause or cure hiccups? Alas, we do not know. But given how often hiccups arise in the Muggle world (from a variety of sources, including eating spicy or hot food or eating food too quickly, laughing raucously, drinking too much alcohol), we can assume that this is a welcome *cure* for the hiccups. Why breathe into a paper bag, turn upside down and drink water, concentrate very hard on getting both index fingers close together (but not touching!), or eating a lemon when you have magic potions at your disposal?

The *Guinness World Records* lists Charles Osborne as the world record holder for the longest attack of hiccups. A few days, you're thinking? A month? Perhaps even an entire year? No, no … Osborne had the hiccups for 68 years! He started hiccupping in 1922, at the age of 28, and finally stopped in 1990, just a year before he died.

Mandrake Restorative Draught

This powerful and important potion restores to normalcy someone who has been petrified, a state in which a person appears to be frozen solid (but is not cold), looks to be in a coma (but has a rigid body), or gives every appearance of being dead (but is actually alive). Someone who is petrified is kept comfortable until the Mandrake Restorative Draught can be concocted, and because the draught calls for only fully grown Mandrakes, the potion can take some time to create.

Chapter 10 gives you the lowdown on the magical properties of the unusual Mandrake plant, the roots of which look initially like a baby, then like a teenager, and later like a fully grown little person. Unlike their human counterparts, however, these Mandrake babies can inflict great physical harm on those trying to harvest the roots.

But this is not all magical lore; the root of this plant really does resemble a small human body. The resemblance is rather eerie; in fact, in the sixteenth and seventeenth centuries, people actually used to clean up Mandrake roots and keep them as little dolls that had magical or psychic powers. They usually hid them, so it wasn't like everyone had Mandrake dolls on their nightstands, but the practice was not unusual.

As for the harm those roots can inflict on the harvester in the Muggle world, Roman legend believed that tiny demons lived in Mandrake roots and would shriek so shrilly at being pulled from the ground that the harvester would die. If you find yourself repotting a wizard Mandrake, perhaps it's better to be safe than sorry—wear ear plugs.

Mandrakes have other wizard uses besides unpetrifying, including untransfiguring someone who has been trapped in an animal's body. Historically, Mandrake in the Muggle world has been used as a pain-killer, aphrodisiac, and a narcotic.

Mrs. Skower's All-Purpose Magical Mess Remover

To "scour" is to clean something by vigorously rubbing or scrub-bing. Mrs. Skower's does the same, cleaning up major messes; it's the OxiClean or Ajax of the wizarding world. Its ingredients are unknown, but an abrasive agent, like nettles, is likely.

Pepperup Potion

This concoction of unknown ingredients works like an Invigoration Draught or Elixir to Induce Euphoria. It's the wizard equivalent of a double espresso or Red Bull.

The closest Muggles have to a true Pepperup Potion is Dr Pepper, which touts itself as the world's oldest major soft drink, created in 1885 in Waco, Texas. Known in the 1950s as "the friendly Pepper-Upper," Dr Pepper was not invented by someone named Dr. Pepper, nor does it contain any pepper, but instead, combines 23 different fruit flavors. One story says that the drink was coined for an actual guy named Dr. Pepper, a friend of the inventor of the drink, Charles Alderton. But the origin of the name remains unclear, so the Dr Pepper Museum in Waco, Texas, tries to sort out the rightful answer. Visit www.drpeppermuseum.org.

Poisons

Poisons are a type of potion meant to maim or kill, and like Muggle poisons, they can be difficult to detect if dropped in a flagon of pumpkin juice or other beverage. To make detection of poisons even more difficult, poisons can be made Undetectable by a skilled wizard.

There are two sure-fire antidotes for poisons known to wizards:

+ *Essence of rue:* Rue is a small, woody, yellow-flowering plant that grows in Europe and Asia, but is not well known in the United States. The oil in its leaves has long been used as both a painkiller and stimulant in the treatment of digestive problems, inflammation, and general malaise, but it can also produce a reaction similar to that of poison ivy and can even be fatal in large doses. The early Greeks used it—just as in the magical world—as an antidote for poisons and to guard against malicious magical spells.

+ *Bezoar:* A bezoar is a small mass, found in the stomach or intestines of some grazing animals, that has long been thought to be an antidote for poisons. In the wizarding world, a bezoar is a stone (think of a kidney stone) taken from the stomach of a goat that, if put down your throat, will save you from most poisons.

Thus, in her two most effective antidotes to lethal poisons, Rowling found her muse in common folklore.

Rowling also mentioned Golpalott's Third Law, which is a brain twister: "The antidote for a blended poison will be equal to more than the sum of the antidotes for each of the separate components." Huh? Apparently, this means that when you mix two poisons together, the antidote has to be stronger than a simple mixing of the two antidotes for each individual potion. We just have to trust that Golpalott ("gulp a lot") knew what he or she was talking about.

Polyjuice Potion

Polyjuice Potion makes you temporarily look like someone else; thus allowing you to take someone's place for a few hours at a time. The potion gets its name from one of its major ingredients, knotgrass, which is from the *Polygonum* genus of the buckwheat family. The prefix poly-also means "more than one"—appropriate, as you are, essentially, "more than one" person after taking this potion.

Polyjuice Potion takes several weeks to make and, in addition to knotgrass, requires shredded boomslang skin, lacewing flies that have been stewed for 21 days, fluxweed that was harvested during a full moon, leeches, and powdered horn of bicorn. As a final ingredient, the potion requires a single hair from the head of the person into whom you are trying to transform.

Shrinking Solution

A Shrinking Solution is the cure for a Swelling Solution or any spell that causes an object to enlarge. Made up of chopped daisy roots, skinned Abyssinian Shrivelfig, sliced caterpillar, rat spleen, and a dash of leech juice, the daisy is the most effective ingredient, as it has long been boiled in milk and fed to farm animals to stunt their growth.

Lewis Carroll's Alice drank a shrinking solution from the "DRINK ME" bottle, which undid the effects of the enlarging "EAT ME" cake. Alice's solution was quite tasty, a mix of "cherry-tart custard, pineapple, roast turkey, toffee, and hot buttered toast." (We can assume that Rowling's mix of caterpillar, rat spleen, and other ingredients is far less palatable.) By taking a little cake, drinking a little solution, again and again, Alice was able to return to her normal size. By alternating a Swelling Solution and Shrinking Solution, perhaps wizards can do the same.

Skele-Gro

Skele-Gro, a potion of unknown ingredients given to wizards who need to regrow one or more bones, is an apt wordplay on a Muggle product called HairGro, which, like its wizarding counterpart, encourages a part of the human body to grow at unusual rates. HairGro has the advantage of being a topical product that is applied to the scalp; Skele-Gro is a horrible steaming potion that burns as it goes down and causes the painful regrowing of bones to commence. It is used not to make wizards taller but to regrow limbs that have been severed or otherwise cursed to no longer have working bones in them.

Scientists at UCLA have isolated a natural molecule that encourages bone growth, but it won't be available as a Muggle potion (er, drug) for another decade.

Sleekeazy's Hair Potion

This potion (ingredients unknown) makes your hair straight and shiny; that is, *sleek*. It is not necessarily *easy* to use, however, as at least one wizard eschews it in favor of a natural, frizzy look. Still, Sleekeazy's is the Garnier Fructis Sleek & Shine of the wizarding world. Note the similarity to the 1920s and 1930s slang "speakeasy," which referred to a place where alcohol could be consumed illegally during Prohibition.

Veritaserum (Truth Potion)

Every culture has its truth serum; intelligence agencies and psychiatrists in the Muggle world have been using Sodium Pentothal, a sedative that causes deep relaxation and loss of inhibition, for decades, so it's no wonder the wizarding world has its own version.

From the Latin *veritas*, meaning truth, and the English *serum*, meaning fluid, this truth-telling potion is so potent that only a few drops lead to spilling your guts. The mere threat of Veritaserum keeps students at Hogwarts in line (see Chapter 8 for more on the wizarding school).

> **MAGIC TALE**
>
> The Latin *veritas* means truth, but with a capital "V" (*Veritas*), it refers to Jesus Christ. Those Romans didn't miss a trick, as Jesus told his followers that he was "the way, the truth, and the light." But one has to wonder why Jesus wasn't referred to as *Via* (way) or *Lumos* (light).

Wit-Sharpening Potion

With scarab beetles as the main ingredient (see the "Insects and Other Creatures" section for more information), this potion doesn't necessarily make you smarter, but it does enhance the intelligence you already have.

Why the scarab beetle? This tiny creature was worshipped by the Egyptians as a symbol of immortality. Unlike the concept of intelligence today, Egyptians believed intelligence took up residence in the heart, not the brain, so after death, Egyptians would remove the deceased's heart, replace it with a scarab beetle carved from stone, place the heart separately in the tomb, and thus ensure that the deceased went into the afterlife with his or her intelligence preserved. No self-respecting Wit-Sharpening Potion would ignore this legacy of intelligence-preservation.

Ginger root is another ingredient of this potion; in the Muggle world, ginger is a major ingredient of teas that are supposed to improve intelligence.

Wolfsbane Potion

Wolfsbane Potion may be the most valuable potion available to wizards: it allows a werewolf to lead a normal life by keeping him or her from transfiguring fully into a werewolf at each full moon—the body still transforms, but the mind doesn't. The potion's main ingredient is aconite (also called monkshood and wolfsbane), a member of the buttercup family that has long been used in small quantities for medicinal purposes—see Chapter 10.

Rowling reveals that this potion was invented by "Damocles Belby." (Belby is a town in East Yorkshire, England.) An earlier Damocles was a Greek royal attendant who upset the ruler at that time, Dionysius, and was repaid by having a sword suspended over his head, held there by a single hair. Thus the term "the sword of Damocles" refers to an impending tragedy, which is exactly how wizards must feel about werewolves. With just one nip, a wizard's entire life is changed: there is no cure, and even though the illness can be kept under control, wizards are so afraid of werewolves that they do everything in their power to push them out of polite society.

Chapter 12

Watch What You Say: Spells, Charms, Hexes, Jinxes, and Curses

In This Chapter

+ Explaining the difference among the terms

+ Understanding how spells work

+ Revealing the power of charms

+ Understanding the more powerful jinxes, hexes, and spells

+ Being aware of the three unforgivable curses

Charms, hexes, jinxes, spells, and curses—along with potions (see Chapter 11)—are a wizard's bread and butter. If you can't toss off a simple tickling charm to torture your little brother, what's the fun in being a wizard? And if you can't protect yourself in a duel, you may as well be a plain-old Muggle.

The various charms, hexes, jinxes, spells, and curses used in the wizarding world are defined in this chapter.

Differentiating Among Charms, Hexes, Jinxes, Spells, and Curses

One of the first questions wizard fans ask is, "What's the difference between a charm, jinx, hex, spell, and curse?" The answer: not much. They're nearly all synonymous.

Charms

The word *charm* is from the Latin *carmen*, meaning song, verse, or prophecy; thus, a charm is a chant, word, or phrase that has magical power. In the world of Harry Potter, charms tend to be rather benign, helping wizards move objects, clean up rooms, improve their physical appearance, and confuse people, rather than physically harm them. Some charms, however, are quite powerful, as you discover in the "Easing In: A Handbook of Charms" section later in this chapter. The Disarming Charm (*Expelliarmus!*) and the Memory Charm (*Obliviate!*) are two good examples.

Note that Rowling overlaps the term *charm* with *spell* or *curse* only twice: A Banishing Spell is also called a Banishing Charm, and an Engorgement Curse is also called an Engorgement Charm.

Hexes

A *hex* is a spell that's meant by the hexer to produce something bad in the hexee. Rowling names only four (Bat-Bogey, Hurling, Stinging, and Twitchy Ears), and all do, indeed, produce ill effects. *Hex* is derived from the German *hexe*, meaning hag or witch. Interestingly, the dictionary lists "hex" and "jinx" as synonyms.

Jinxes

A *jinx* is another word for a hex—a spell that produces an ill effect. A jinx is never benign and is used for two reasons:

1. To counter the spells or activities of someone else, as is the case with Anti-Disapparition and Anti-intruder jinxes

2. To incapacitate an enemy, such is the case with Jelly-Legs and Impediment jinxes

Rowling points out that the word "counterjinx" is a misnomer: because jinxes, by definition, are often used to counter other spells, "counterjinx" and "jinx" are synonymous. Jinxes and curses are even similar enough to share terminology: the Impediment Jinx is also referred to as the Impediment Curse in the novels, making it a serious spell indeed.

Magic Tale

The origin of the word "jinx" is found in Greek mythology. Iynx, the daughter of Pan and Peitho, tried to use magic to make Zeus fall in love with her (note that there is no such love spell in the wizarding world; see Chapter 11 for love potions). In retribution, Hera turned Iynx into a bird called the iynx (also called the Iynx and the wryneck bird). So, in a way, Hera jinxed Iynx!

Spells

Spell is the default term that encompasses all charms, hexes, jinxes, and curses. From the Old English *spel*, meaning story or account, a spell has come to mean any word or phrase with magical power. Note, in fact, the way we use both *charm* and *spell* in everyday usage—for example, a *charming* man can cast a *spell* on a woman. Both have the sense of magical power, irresistibility, or enchantment. Spells can be benign (like most charms) or severe (like hexes, jinxes, and curses). Only once does Rowling officially call a spell something else, however: the Banishing Spell is also referred to as a Banishing Charm.

Curses

In Harry Potter's world, a *curse* is a high-level spell that usually produces great discomfort in the victim. By definition, a curse is used to call evil down on another (it's from the Old English *curs*, meaning prayer or malediction), so it makes sense that a curse isn't used to stir a pot of mashed potatoes or clean your dishes, the way a charm might be. Good wizards do occasionally utilize curses, but almost exclusively in self-defense. Evil wizards, on the other hand, might use a dozen curses before breakfast. See the "Mastering the Minor Curses" section for details on specific curses.

Three curses are considered Unforgivable, although some of the so-called minor curses can produce results nearly as bad as the Unforgivables. See the "Steering Clear of the Three Unforgivable Curses" section later in this chapter.

Understanding How Spells Are Named and Produced

Spells have both a name and an *incantation*, which is the word or words a wizard speaks to produce the spell. In order for the spell to work, the wizard must speak (or, for really advanced wizards, *think*) the incantation, often in conjunction with some sort of wand movement. It is possible, however, for some spells to be produced in the absence of a wand. These tend to occur when a very powerful wizard is under extreme stress or is enraged.

In Rowling's novels, incantations are given in italics, followed by an exclamation point (incantations must be said with feeling, and the exclamation point communicates this). That same convention is followed in this chapter.

In some cases, only the name of the spell is mentioned in the H*arry Potter* novels; in others, Rowling gives only the incantation; and in still other cases, Rowling gives us both the name and the incantation. So you'll see some inconsistencies—not every spell has an incantation, and vice versa.

Easing In: A Handbook of Charms

Most—although not all—charms are fun, harmless ways of using magic. In an ideal world, wizards would use only charms, not the more danger-ous hexes, jinxes, spells, and curses. For this reason, Charms is a class taught at Hogwarts (see Chapter 8); the more aggressive spells are not taught at school, although defending against them is taught.

Hogwarts also offers a Charm Club, which is something on par with a Muggle Debate Club or French Club. Mostly a social club, it is also an opportunity to practice rendering charms.

Accio! (Summoning Charm)

This charms fetches whatever you need—even through locked doors, if necessary. Lose your keys? No problem. Do a quick summoning spell, and they'll come to your hand. Leave your lunch at home? Same deal. As long as you follow *Accio!* with the name of the object you want, it'll come to you. *Accio*, not surprisingly, is Latin for send for or summon.

Aguamenti Charm

This charm makes water stream or whoosh from the tip of a wand, which could be pretty handy on a hot, sunny day. *Agua* is Spanish for water; *mentis* is Latin for intention.

Alohomora! (Alohomora Charm)

This incredibly handy charm opens locks on doors and windows—no more calling AAA to get your keys out of your car; no more climbing in a window when you're locked out of the house.

In one of the more clever naming schemes of all charms and spells, *aloha* is the Hawaiian word for "goodbye" (it also is used to mean "hello"), and *mora* is Latin for obstacle or hindrance. Goodbye, obstacle; hello, unlocked door!

Confundus Charm

From the Latin *confunudi*, meaning to confuse or bewilder, this charm is meant to confuse someone temporarily. If a wizard runs into an old classmate on the street and doesn't have time to chat, a Confundus Charm that lasts for thirty seconds would be just enough time to make a clean getaway.

Expelliarmus! (Disarming Charm)

From the Latin *expello*, meaning to expel or reject, this charm is used mostly to de-wand another wizard. Without a wand, a wizard's powers are greatly inhibited, so separating a wizard from his wand is like getting a gun away from an opponent.

Homorphus Charm

From the Latin *homo* (man) and the English *morph* (to change from one thing into another), this powerful charm is supposed to force a werewolf to turn back into a human. Given how dangerous werewolves are and how useful a charm like this would be, this charm probably does not actually work; the wizard describing its existence in the novels has not proven to be a reliable source.

Imperturbable Charm

Need to have a private conversation without anyone eavesdropping? A wizard would use an Imperturbable Charm, which Imperturbs an object to create a privacy barrier. (The English *imperturbable* means calm, undisturbed, and not easily distressed.) Doors are the primary targets, but entire walls could be Imperturbed.

Impervius!

From the Latin (and English) *impervious*, meaning impermeable, this incantation does not allow one substance to penetrate another. For example, a wizard can charm an object to repel water. Perhaps Dockers stain-resistant pants were designed with the *Impervius!* incantation.

Locomotor!

The verb *locomote*, from which we get the word *locomotive* (train), means to move under your own power. Not surprisingly, this incantation is used to move objects, like a heavy suitcase. Like *Accio!*, the incantation must be followed by the name of the object.

Lumos!

From the Latin *lumen*, meaning light, this incantation produces light at the end of the wand, helping one to see in the dark.

Nox!

From the Latin *nox*, meaning darkness, this incantation causes the light at the end of the wand to go out. It is used as a countercharm to *Lumos!*

Obliteration Charm

The Obliteration Charm ("to obliterate" means to erase completely, leaving no trace) is used to make the traces of anything disappear, including footsteps in the snow.

Obliviate! (Memory Charm)

This incantation is from the Latin *oblivio*, meaning forgetfulness, with is the root of the English *oblivious* (unaware and/or forgetful) and *oblivion* (the state of having been forgotten). The Memory Charm is used most often on Muggles, forcing them to forget the wizard activities they may have accidentally seen; it modifies a person's memory. It can also be used wizard-to-wizard to make someone forget something damaging or embarrassing. A wizard could, conceivably, even forget a painful breakup like in *Eternal Sunshine of the Spotless Mind* by using this charm.

Protean Charm

The Protean Charm is one of the coolest—and most difficult—charms a wizard can perform, and it requires great skill. From the word *protean*, which means continually changing in appearance or behavior, this charm allows a wizard to make a change to one base item, and then any items associated with that item will change in the same way. For example, a group of everyday items, such as quills, are bewitched to change color, shape, or some other characteristic when the wizard changes the main quill. In this way, clandestine messages can be given to a group of wizards. The Dark Mark that Lord Voldemort gives to each of his followers is likely powered by the Protean Charm.

Magic Tale

Proteus was a Greek sea god who could foretell the future, but only to those who could catch him. Because he was a shapeshifter, catching him was no easy task. Proteus could take the forms of many animals and several bodies of water (streams, lakes, seas).

Protego! (Shield Charm)

From the Latin *protego*, meaning protect and defend, the Shield Charm deflects minor spells and rebounds them on the attacker. The charm creates a temporary force field around the wizard issuing this incantation.

Relashio!

Probably from the Latin *relatio*, meaning motion, this charm sends something—perhaps sparks—out of the end of a wand and slightly wounds the person at whom the wand is aimed.

Reparo!

From the Latin *reparo*, meaning repair, this charm repairs something broken: a mug; a pair of glasses; the iPod you dropped on the sidewalk; the large dent in your car.

Silencio! (Silencing Charm)

From the Latin *silens*, meaning silent, this charm forces someone to quiet down. It's the wizard equivalent of using your "indoor voice" when in kindergarten. The charm may require a sharp poke from the wand, but that's probably just to get the attention of the loud talker.

Sonorus!

From the Latin (and English) *sonorous*, meaning a loud, deep, clear sound, this useful charm, evoked by pointing a wand at one's own throat, turns a normal voice into a megaphone voice.

Tergeo!

From the Latin *tergeo*, meaning to clean or polish, this charm is used to clean dirt, blood, or any other goo off one's body or clothing.

Rictusempra! (Tickling Charm)

The is the ultimate charm in a sibling's toolkit, because it allows a wizard to tickle someone without even having to get his or her fingers near another person's tummy. The Latin *rictus* means open mouth or jaw, *semper* means always; hence, always laughing.

Waddiwasi!

This charm shoots a "wad" of gum (and, presumably, other objects) up someone's nose. Perhaps that's where the incantation originates; if not, the origin of this incantation is difficult to pin down:

+ *Waddi* is a rare tree in the Australian Outback that grows right alongside the gum tree.

+ *Vadd* is Swedish for soft cotton.

+ *Wasi* means house in the Native American language of Quechua.

+ *Vas-y* means "you go" in French. The best fit is wad + *vas-y*, to mean "you go, wad!"

Wingardium Leviosa! (Levitating Charm)

This charm, one of the first learned by students at Hogwarts, causes objects to rise into the air. The first word of the incantation is likely derived from the English *wing* and the Latin *arduus*, meaning steep or high. The second word may be derived from two Latin sources: *levo*, meaning lift (but usually more in the sense of "supporting") and *levitas*, meaning lightness. Hence, this incantation is about raising something light up high, as if with wings. The charm appears to be used to lift objects; a wizard wanting to levitate people would use the *Levicorpus!* incantation.

Moving Up to More Challenging Hexes, Jinxes, and Spells

As I've mentioned, there is virtually no difference between a hex and a jinx; both tend to produce painful results and are not considered "nice" in the wizarding world. Jinxes, however, are often used defensively, either to deflect a spell or to incapacitate a dangerous wizard. Hexes are almost always used offensively, and one can work to gain proficiency in deflecting hexes.

A spell can be of the benign, charm-like variety or may be as deadly as a curse. *Spell* is the default term that is used synonymously with charm, hex, jinx, and curse.

Anapneo!

This incantation saves a person from choking; it's the wizard equivalent of the Heimlich Maneuver. It is derived from the Greek *apapneo* (breathe), from which we get the English word apnea, which is a temporary suspension of breathing. (Sleep apnea is a condition in which a person stops breathing for a few seconds several times during the night.)

Aparecium!

From the Latin *aperio*, meaning to show or discover, this incantation forces invisible ink to become visible.

Avis!

From the Latin *avis*, meaning bird, this incantation makes birds shoot out of the end of a wand.

Bat-Bogey Hex

This hex is great to use on an opponent, because it covers his or her face with large, flapping bats that presumably were formed from the person's bogies. This hex may also be known as the Curse of the Bogies, a curse that is mentioned but not defined in Rowling's novels.

KING'S ENGLISH

A **bogey** in the United States is a frightening object; for example, a bogey-man (often spelled "boogie man") is the monster that hides under the bed or in the closet. But in the UK, bogey generally has one meaning: booger.

Colloportus!

Probably derived from the Latin *colligo* (connect) and *portus* (harbor or haven), this spell seals a door together with a loud squish, the way a boot sounds in mud. The spell, therefore, creates an airtight seal.

Densaugeo!

From the Latin *dens*, meaning tooth, and *augeo*, meaning increase, this incantation causes teeth to grow at any alarming rate.

Diffindo!

From the Latin *diffindo*, meaning split, this spell causes something to split or break—another person's pants, a bookbag, and so on.

Ennervate!

This incantation has an interesting history in Rowling's novels. It is used to revive someone who has fainted, been knocked out, or been Stunned, yet the definition of "enervate" is to *weaken* someone's vitality, not to strengthen it, which means that the incantation is a word that means the opposite of the incantation's outcome. So, Rowling renamed this incantation *Rennervate!* ("unweaken"), which matches the purpose of the spell much more closely.

Episkey! (Healing Spell)

From the Greek *episkeyazo*, meaning to recondition or repair, this Healing Spell restores an injured wizard back to health.

Evanesco! (Vanishing Spell)

From the Latin *evanesco*, meaning disappear, this spell makes an object vanish. The larger and more complex the object, the more difficult the spell is to perform. Making the broccoli on your plate vanish doesn't take much skill; disappearing a house takes a substantial amount of wizarding power.

Ferula!

A *ferule* is a spanking paddle, and *Ferula communis* is the botanical name for giant fennel, which has huge stalks that are strong and wide. We can assume, then, that Rowling was referring to a splint of some kind when using the incantation *Ferula!*, because this spell splints and bandages up a break or sprain.

Finite Incantatem!

Finite means "end," and *Incantatem!* refers to incantations; thus, this spell stops all spells. This is what you say when your wizard children have been playing in the backyard all morning, hexing and jinxing each other, and you've had enough.

Flagrate!

From the Latin *flagro*, meaning blaze or flame, this incantation affixes a large, flaming "X" on an object, making it easy to find and recognize in the future.

Incendio!

From the word *incendiary*, meaning highly flammable, this incantation creates fire.

Langlock!

Likely derived from the English words *language* and *lock*, this incantation glues the tongue to the roof of the mouth, rendering the person unable to speak (and, thus, language is locked).

Leberacorpus!

This incantation undoes *Levicorpus!* (see the following entry), bringing a body back down to the ground. It's likely derived from the Latin *liber* (free or unimpede) and *corpus* (body).

Levicorpus!

From the Latin *levis*, meaning light, and *corpus*, meaning body, this incantation levitates a body. Different from *Wingardium Leviosa!* (the Levitating Charm) because it's lifting a human being, and none too carefully. Differentiate this spell also from the *Mobilcorpus!* curse, in which a person is being controlled like a puppet, while dangling above the ground.

Mobiliarbus!

Wizards with a green thumb can make great use of this incantation, which moves a tree from one place to another. The incantation is derived from the Latin *mobilis*, meaning movable, and *arbor*, meaning tree.

Oppugno!

From the Latin *oppugno*, meaning assault or attack, this none-too-friendly charm provokes something (birds, for example) to attack another wizard. The effect isn't deadly or even injury-inducing, but it is annoying and perhaps even frightening. This could be the incantation for the Bat-Bogey Hex, but the two are never connected in the *Harry Potter* novels.

Portus!

From the Latin *porta*, meaning gate or entrance and *portus*, meaning harbor, haven, or port, this spell creates a Portkey, which is a transportation device (see Chapter 5).

Serpensortia!

From the Latin *serpens*, meaning serpent and *ortus/orior* (to have appeared on the scene), this incantation causes a snake to shoot out of the end of a wand.

Specialis Revelio! (Scarpin's Revelaspell)

This spell identifies the ingredients of a potion, allowing one to sniff out poisons, truth serum, love potions, and other dangerous concoctions. The spell also allows a wizard to detect unique ingredients in potions, thus copying them. (See Chapter 11 for more on potions.) The incantation is derived from the English words *special* and *reveal*. Using it on something other than a potion can sometimes reveal some history or secret of that object.

Stupefy! (Stunning Spell)

Stupefy! is an extremely effective spell when in a fight, because it temporarily disables your attacker, producing roughly the same effect as using a stun gun. From *stupor*, which comes from the Latin *stupeo*, meaning stunned or numbed, this spell is colloquially referred to in the wizarding world as a Stunner.

Tarantallegra!

This spell causes one to tap dance frantically. The incantation is a combination of the *tarantella*, a fast-moving Italian dance, and the Italian word *allegro*, meaning fast or high-spirited.

TOURIST TIP

Visit the city of Taranto, in southern Italy, where the tarantella originated and is still practiced in some weddings and even in town festivals. This couples' dance begins slowly, and then changes direction each time the music, played on a mandolin, speeds up. Before long, keeping up is nearly impossible. Legend has it that the tarantella began in the Middle Ages to help sweat out the effects of a tarantula bite, which was thought to be poisonous (it usually isn't).

Mastering the Minor Curses

Although no curse should be considered "minor," compared to the Unforgivable Curses (which allow for stealing a person's identity, torturing a person, or killing a person), even the dangerous curses in this section may seem benign.

Furnunculus! (Furnunculus Curse)

In what probably fits in the category of "vocabulary you didn't ever need to know," *carbuncle* is the medical term for a pimple, and a *furuncle* is a boil. Thus, this curse causes huge boils to spring up on the victim.

Impedimentia! (Impediment Curse)

This curse (also called a jinx) slows down, obstructs, and even stops attackers, making it extremely useful when dueling or battling. If you're running away and can throw an Impediment Curse over your shoulder, you'll gain the advantage. It's derived from the Latin *impedimentum*, meaning hindrance or impediment.

Incarcerous!

From *incarcerate* (to imprison), this incantation places ropes around a person's arms and legs, temporarily securing the prisoner.

Locomotor Mortis! (Leg-Locker Curse)

The English verb *locomote* means to move under your own power. *Mortis* is Latin for death. "Death to moving under your own power" is a great way to describe what happens with the Leg-Locker Curse, which locks a person's legs together, bunny-hop style, and renders him partially paralyzed.

Mobilcorpus!

From the Latin *mobilis*, meaning movable and changeable, and *corpus*, meaning body, this incantation makes a person or object as malleable as a puppet, able to be moved and controlled for a period of time.

Morsmordre!

From the Latin *mors* (death) and the French *mordre* (to bite), this frightening incantation causes Lord Voldemort's Dark Mark (an intertwining skull and snake, in glowing green) to hover in the sky. Lord Voldemort's goal is to defeat death and achieve immortality; hence, "to bite death."

Reducto! (Reductor Curse)

From the Latin *reductus*, meaning receding deeply, this curse reduces items to a fraction of their original size. Don't want to go around that park bench on your walk? Use the Reductor Curse! Tired of hitting your head on that low-hanging beam? Blast it out of sight! This curse also works as an antidote to the Engorgement Curse.

Sectumsempra!

From the Latin *sectum* (cut) and *sempra* (always), this ghastly incantation is used in battle to cover one's enemy in deep cuts. This is a serious, powerful curse that can cause great damage.

Magic Tale

The U.S. Marine Corps has a Latin motto that would do a wizard proud: *Semper Fidelis* (often shortened to *Semper Fi*), and both terms are used in Rowling's spells. (*Semper* means always; *Fidelis* means faithful.) The British Royal Marines also boast a Latin motto: *Per Mare Per Terram* (by sea, by land), but no wizard spells contain those Latin words.

Transmogrifian Torture

This curse may exist only in the minds of braggart wizards, but if it *is* real, it can kill someone. That it exists is unlikely, because it would clearly be included among the Unforgivable Curses.

The origin of *Transmogrifian* is not entirely clear, although *mogrify* is a computer programming term for transforming an image. And, of course, Calvin (of the famed *Calvin and Hobbes* comic strip) had a Transmogrifier machine.

Steering Clear of the Three Unforgivable Curses

Aptly named, these curses are unforgivable. Using any of them on another person will, if caught, lead to a life sentence in Azkaban prison (see Chapter 15). They're listed here in order of their impact on the victim.

Imperio! (Imperious Curse)

From the Latin *impero*, meaning command or rule over, this curse gives the curser total control over the victim. Whatever the wizard who is in command orders of the other person, the person under the Imperius Curse must obediently perform.

Those with very strong personalities can fight off this curse, and when doing so, the actions and speech of the victim will be jerky and hesitant until the curse can be thrown off completely.

Crucio! (Cruciatus Curse)

From the Latin *crucio*, meaning torture, this curse causes unbelievable agony for the victim. There's no need for thumbscrews in the wizarding world; one jolt of this curse and the victim will jerk, shudder, and twitch from unbelievable pain. People have gone insane from this curse. Like any torture, it can get people to talk if a truth potion (see Chapter 11) isn't close at hand.

Avada Kedavra! (Killing Curse)

In the wizarding world, no one has to use guns or bombs to kill someone; instead, this curse does the job. Because the curse can be performed only by powerful wizards and requires a strong presence of magic, there is no blocking it. And there's no countercurse, either. Only one person (Harry Potter) has ever survived it.

The incantation is a play on *abracadabra*, the age-old incantation for any spell desired, and on *cadaver*, meaning corpse.

Chapter 13

Advanced Wizardry

In This Chapter

+ Changing your appearance at will

+ Enlisting the help of a protector

+ Looking beyond symbols

+ Reading someone's mind and emotions

+ Becoming a prophesier

+ Speaking with snakes

+ Keeping a secret and a promise

+ Saving your soul

Beyond the herbology, potions, and spells discussed in the previous three chapters, the greatest wizards practice advanced magic that ranges from morphing the shapes of their bodies to getting inside another wizard's thoughts to conversing with snakes ... and the most evil of all advanced wizardry, splitting one's soul in an attempt to achieve immortality. This chapter gives you the lowdown on what the best (or worst) and brightest wizards are up to.

Being an Animagus or Metamorphmagus

Advanced wizards can change their appearance at will (that is, without the help of a wand or potion):

+ An *Animagus*, combining ani (from animal) with *magus* (Latin for magician), is a wizard who can transform into the shape of an animal at will. This difficult skill can be learned. For werewolves (see Chapter 2), the transformation happens without the control or consent of the person, so a werewolf is not considered an Animagus.

+ A *Metamorphmagus* (meta means "change" or "alteration," morph means "form") is a wizard who can change appearance at will. This is not a skill that can be learned, although wizards can change a portion of their appearance—such as the size of their teeth—with spells or potions (but the effects might be temporary). Metamorphmagi are born with the skill.

An Animagus takes only one animal or insect form (cat, dog, deer, rat, or beetle, for example), and that form often resembles the human in some way. Because Animagi are unrecognizable as humans, however, and because an Animagus transformation is difficult magic that's fraught with danger, all Animagi must register with the Ministry of Magic, indicating what sort of animal they transform into and what that animal's particular markings are. Failure to register is considered a serious crime.

Powerful wizards can return an Animagus to his human form, even against his will. This practice allows unregistered and/or criminal Animagi to be exposed as their true selves.

A Metamorphmagus, on the other hand, does not need to register the skill of changing hair length and color, nose shape and size, and eye shape and color.

Shapeshifting is certainly not new in literature; in fact, it is one of the most common abilities among gods, wizards, fairies, elves, and others in mythology and fantasy, especially in Celtic lore but also in the following:

+ Ged, the young wizard in Ursula Le Guin's *The Wizard of Earthsea*, can transform into a hawk.

+ In Patrice Kindl's *Owl in Love*, a 13-year-old girl transforms into an owl at night.

+ Merlin turns young Arthur (before he becomes king) into several different animals in T.H. White's *The Sword in the Stone*, so that Arthur can learn from the animals.

+ Similarly, in Christopher Paolini's *Eldest*, Eragon learns the nature of the universe by inserting himself into the minds of animals, from ants to squirrels, and viewing the world through their eyes.

+ In C.S. Lewis's *The Voyage of the Dawn Treader*, Eustace is turned into a dragon for a time, and through this experience becomes an almost nice person.

+ In Caribbean and African folktales, young men regularly turn into birds, insects, and animals of all sizes and shapes.

+ In the Grimm Brothers' "Hans, My Hedgehog" and "Beauty and the Beast," the love of a woman transforms a beast into his beautiful human self. In fact, princes and princesses are regularly turned into frogs, beasts, and other animals as the result of a punishing spell, and these effects are temporary until the proper conditions exist for the reversal of that spell.

+ In the movie *Shrek*, a princess takes the form of an ogre each night. In both versions of Disney's *The Shaggy Dog*, men are turned into sheepdogs, and hilarity ensues.

+ Mythological gods and goddesses often took animal forms, and just as often, they punished others by turning them into animals.

+ Apuleius's *The Golden Ass*, Ovid's *Metamorphoses*, and Homer's *The Odyssey* all contain instances of humans transforming into animals.

Conjuring a Patronus

When faced with a dementor (a guard at Azkaban prison; see Chapter 15), an exceptional wizard can perform a Patronus Charm. *Patronus* is derived from the word patron, which means protector or defender (from the Latin *patrius*, for father), and in the wizarding world, a Patronus acts as a defender against a dementor.

A Patronus, which takes a unique animal shape for the wizard conjuring it, isn't bothered by the happiness-sucking practice of dementors.

To conjure a Patronus, a wizard must think about a very happy memory (or even a happy daydream), and then utter the incantation *Expecto Patronum!* A silver vapor then emanates from the wizard's wand, and that vapor turns into the Patronus, which is life size, but shiny, silvery, and almost ghostlike. Wizards who are still learning the Patronus Charm produce only the silvery smoke, while more advanced wizards produce a corporeal (that is, a visible and tangible) Patronus.

Patron saints are an important feature of Catholicism and resemble a Patronus in some ways. (Saints are holy people who, when they lived, had unusual relationships with God; in Catholicism, the formal process of canonization—that is, sainthood—takes years to complete.) Patron saints, because of their individual histories, represent a particular condition (physical or spiritual), state, or vocation, and Catholics ask for intercession on the part of that patron saint when praying. So, for example, an athlete might, in prayer, ask Saint Sebastian, the patron saint of athletes, to pray for him or her to help with an injury or because of a difficult upcoming match, acting as a sort of protector. (Note that patron saints are not gods or deities; asking a patron saint to pray on one's behalf is like asking a next-door neighbor to pray on one's behalf. No one would suggest that the person believes the next-door neighbor is a god. The only difference is that the patron saint happens to be dead.)

Similarly, in religious practices throughout history, a guardian angel is a protector like a Patronus. Artifacts show that Babylonians and Assyrians believed in the presence of angels who guarded people from harm and helped them succeed. Both the Old and New Testaments also reference angels who protect people from harm.

Deciphering Runes

The study of runes—that is, symbols that make up a 24-character alphabet known as the Futhark—does not have a significant place in the wizarding world of Harry Potter. Only one main character (Hermione Granger) is known to study the subject; she is often caught reading books like *Ancient Runes Made Easy*, *Magical Hieroglyphs and Logograms*, *Advanced Rune Translations*, as well as referencing a rune dictionary.

Runes have, however, had a place in British culture since the collapse of Rome and the Age of Migrations (also called the Dark Ages). Originally derived from Greek, runes were used by Germanic and Scandinavian settlers in Britain after the Romans left the area, roughly around 300 to 400 c.e. The 24 original runic symbols (9 more were added a few hundred years after their first use, but they're considered to be posers) are as follows:

ᚠ	Fehu	ᚱ	Raido
ᚢ	Uraz	ᚲ	Kauno
ᚦ	Thurisaz	ᚷ	Gebo
ᚨ	Ansuz	ᚹ	Wunjo

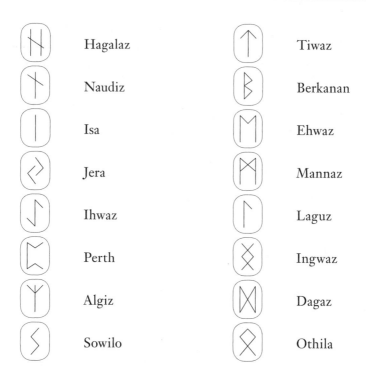

Hagalaz	Tiwaz
Naudiz	Berkanan
Isa	Ehwaz
Jera	Mannaz
Ihwaz	Laguz
Perth	Ingwaz
Algiz	Dagaz
Sowilo	Othila

However, runes are not simply an alphabet of letters that are combined to make words; their study and understanding is far more complex. Each rune is made up of a symbol that is not only beautiful in and of itself but also has a direct translation, a meaning (an expansion of the translation), a personal interpretation for your own life, characteristics that further examine the translation and meaning, a tie to the natural world of animals and plants, a number, a color, an element (fire, earth, water, air), a polarity (male or female), associated gods, correspondence to an astrological sign, correspondence to a Tarot card, a reverse meaning, and a converse meaning.

Magic Tale

Use of the word "rune" abounds in dragon literature and modern fantasy. The word, even if readers aren't exactly sure what it means when they see it, conjures up images of secrecy and magic. Christopher Paolini mentions runes dozens of times in the lengthy novels *Eragon* and *Eldest*, and the meaning is roughly the idea of "letters of an alphabet." In those novels, 11 runes are the oldest and most unique; dwarf runes are quite similar to human runes, humans having based their alphabet on that of the dwarves.

With so much meaning attributed to each runic symbol, runes have long been used in divination—that is, to tell one's personal fortune. They have had other magical uses, too, including casting spells and weaving charms.

Using Legilimency and Occlumency

Legilimency is the practice of reading someone's thoughts, memories, and emotions, usually for nefarious purposes, although it is sometimes done with good intentions. Eye contact makes the practice much easier. The greatest Legilimens is Lord Voldemort, the Dark Lord himself, who has a Legilimenian connection with Harry Potter; they can sometimes share thoughts and feelings without even trying (and, indeed, against their wills).

The term literally means the state of reading the mind (the Latin *legens* means "reading," the Latin *mens* means "mind," and the suffix *-ency* means "the state of"), but Legilimency is far subtler than simply reviewing the thoughts in a person's head. A skilled Legilimens can determine the intentions of the person, and so can determine whether a person has just lied, is going to betray those around him, or has intentions other than those he has stated.

Occlumency is the antidote to Legilimency. Literally meaning "the state of closing the mind" (*occludo* is Latin for shut up or close), Occlumency can keep even a skilled Legilimens from penetrating the mind. The key to becoming a skilled Occlumens is to make the mind as blank as possible, thus revealing nothing about your intentions, emotions, and thoughts.

Knowing what's in the hearts and minds of others is an oft-used device in literature, but that knowledge tends to come more from intuition and the character and tendencies of another and less from directly reading one's thoughts. True mind-probing is relatively uncommon in literature, but two such examples come to mind: in Christopher Paolini's *Eragon* and *Eldest*, mind-probing is common among Dragon Riders, who also learn to shut out the probes of others. Dragon Riders can also scry others, which means they can check up on people and places they have seen before (they cannot scry something they have yet to see), even if the other person or place is at a great distance. And, of course, Mr. Spock was expert at the Vulcan mind meld in the original *Star Trek* TV series—in close proximity, often touching another person's forehead, a Vulcan can share the thoughts, knowledge, experiences, and memories of the other.

Practicing Prophecy

Divination is the practice of attempting to predict the future; a divination (or prophecy) is also the name given to a particular prediction of the future. A Seer (one with the Inner Eye) makes prophecies, while an Object is one about whom a prophecy is made.

Divination is one of the few foundations that nearly all cultures share, from Mesopotamia and Babylonia to the Greeks and Romans, continuing throughout the history of Western civilization, and including Eastern cultures such as China and Korea. Divination was not considered "evil" or "alternative" as it is in many cultures now, but an important component of spiritual and religious life. Even the birth and death of Jesus were foretold as prophecy.

In the wizarding world, however, divination is generally treated with a bit of, er, skepticism. Hogwarts' Divination teacher, Sibyll Trelawney, is considered by many to be a fraud. Sibyll (*sibyl* is Greek for "wise" or "prophetic") spends her time teaching students to interpret tea leaves, look into crystal balls, read cards, interpret dreams, and review the flight pattern of birds, none of which a true Seer needs in order to prophesize. Trelawney not only teaches Divination through such tools but also uses them to makes vague predictions of doom that few pay any attention to. She insists that her gifts are legitimate, perhaps insisting a bit too vehemently. One wonders whether the Divination teacher has any real confidence in her abilities.

However, Trelawney is the descendent of a truly gifted Seer and, in moments she does not later recall—and without the aid of any of the Divination tools on which she relies—Trelawney utters meaningful prophecies. Such prophecies (and others, revealed by other Seers) are stored in glass orbs in the Hall of Prophecy in the Department of Mysteries at the Ministry of Magic (see Chapter 14). As long as the orbs remain unbroken, prophecies can be played back like a tape recorder. Prophecies can also be repeated by anyone who overhears them.

Prophecies do, indeed, predict what *can* happen in the future. But this is where they get interesting. Prophecies are not glimpses of the future. They are not plays that actors will soon act out, like puppets on a string. Instead, everyone involved in the prophecy is free to ignore it and go about his or her life. But because most people act on the prophecy—fearing, or, conversely, desiring its outcome—the prophecy is often fulfilled.

Magic Tale

Myth and folktales are filled with examples of people who, upon hearing a prophecy, acted on it to avoid its coming true, but instead succeeded only in creating perfect conditions in which the prophecy could happen. Consider the story of Oedipus, whose father was told that Oedipus would kill him and marry Oedipus's mother. Terrified of this prophecy, Oedipus's father created the very conditions under which the prophecy could be fulfilled: he injured his son and sent him out into the wilderness to die. Oedipus was saved by a servant and, never knowing his father or mother, eventually fulfilled the prophecy. Had the father chosen not to act on the prophecy and to raise Oedipus as his son, odds are the boy would never have killed his father or been attracted to his mother.

Such is the case with the essential prophecy around which Harry Potter and Lord Voldemort center their lives. Trelawney predicted that a boy born in July to parents who had defied Voldemort three times would have the power to vanquish the Dark Lord, and that either the boy or Voldemort must die at the hands of the other. Now, if Voldemort had left this alone, it may or may not have come true. But, like Oedipus's father, he acted on it, choosing Harry as that boy, even though another boy fit the description equally. In so choosing Harry, he marked the boy, and thus set the fulfillment of the prophecy in motion.

Perhaps the best-known prophet in history was Pythia, the priestess of a shrine to Apollo, called Delphi, that was located at the center of the Greek world. Known as the Oracle at Delphi, Pythia communicated with Apollo and shared his prophecies. They were vague and subject to all sorts of interpretation, but heads of state and more common folk alike consulted the Oracle for guidance. In Roman times, pure prophecy in the trance-like state into which Pythia fell was replaced with more assistive forms of prophecy, such as those practiced by Sibyll Trelawney.

Speaking in Parseltongue

A Parselmouth—that is, one who can talk to snakes—speaks in the language of Parseltongue, which is made up of hissing sounds. It tends to be a talent one simply possesses, and it is not taught—nor for that matter, used—at Hogwarts.

Traditionally, the ability to speak Parseltongue has been the mark of a Dark Wizard. In fact, the ability has been associated with Salazar

Slytherin, founder of Slytherin House at Hogwarts (see Chapter 8), the house that has produced more Dark Wizards than any other. Lord Voldemort, the darkest of all wizards, is the best-known Parselmouth. However, not all Parselmouths are evil, as Harry Potter speaks fluent Parseltongue. His ability to hear snakes has saved the day on more than one occasion.

According to an interview with J.K. Rowling, Parselmouth is an "old word for someone who has a problem with their mouth," as with a harelip.

Snakes have never been well-liked in culture and literature. A snake was, after all, responsible for the fall of man, when a serpent tempted Eve into tasting the forbidden fruit. Serpent mythology and folktales, in fact, are among the most recognizable cultural stories in the world. Both feared and respected, serpents were thought to be the most dangerous of all creatures, but they have been used in both healing and fertility rites.

Serpents have been associated with gods and goddesses and played a role in a variety of literature, from Mesopotamian mythology and the Babylonian *Epic of Gilgamesh* to Kipling's *The Jungle Book*.

Sealing the Deal with a Fidelius Charm or an Unbreakable Vow

A Fidelius Charm, rarely mentioned in the wizarding world, is a complicated charm that hides information inside a person, who is known as a Secret-Keeper. (*Fidelis* is Latin for faithful, loyal, trustworthy, and dependable.) As long as the Secret-Keeper says nothing, it is impossible for anyone else to discover that information, even if faced with it directly before him. So if you wanted to know the location of a soccer game, but that information had been hidden inside a Secret-Keeper, you wouldn't be able to find that soccer game even if you walked onto the soccer pitch (field) and tripped over the players themselves.

However, if the Secret-Keeper divulges the secret, the charm is nullified, and the hidden information is up for grabs. Because of the power of Dark Wizards to perform Legilimency, Secret-Keeping is important business. Wizards must always choose their Secret-Keepers carefully; their very lives could depend on it.

An Unbreakable Vow is similar to a Fidelius Charm, but instead of a secret that cannot be learned, it represents a vow that cannot be broken ... ever. To make such an airtight vow, the two people making the vow take each other's right hands while a third party, a Bonder, stands over them. The vow is said out loud, while a flame surrounds the two vow-makers' hands. It's the equivalent of the fidelity claimed by blood brothers, but with much less spit and blood and with a much greater consequence if the vow is broken.

What happens if you break the vow? Simple: you die. Imagine if a bride and groom took this approach. The divorce rate would surely decrease, but the number of deaths might increase somewhat!

Creating a Horcrux

A Horcrux is, perhaps, the most difficult to understand—and the most evil—of all advanced wizardry. There is only one reason to create a Horcrux, and that is to achieve immortality.

A Horcrux is an object in which you hide a portion of your soul. If, after you've created a Horcrux, your body is killed, you will survive because that hidden portion of your soul will remain untouched. You can then rebuild your body, starting with the torn portion of your soul.

It's not the attempt at immortality that makes the creation of a Horcrux inherently evil; instead, it is the means by which the soul is torn. A soul is split in only one way: by committing the act of murder. This act is so evil that it rips the soul, and thus allows the split portion to be stored in a Horcrux. A split soul will be a lesser soul, however, because the human soul was meant to remain whole and unblemished.

The word *Horcrux* likely derives from Latin words. The English word crucible, a container that can resist both great heat and withstand a severe test or trial, is associated with the Latin *crux*. And *hor* is likely a shortened version of several Latin terms that all lead to the English horror, horrid, and horrible. Thus, a Horcrux is a "horror-filled container," which is an apt term for a container holding the portions of a person's soul ripped apart by committing murder.

Dualism of the soul is an idea long present in the Bible, in which a soul is thought to be immortal, while the body is not. "Soul" is often used as a synonym for "life" in the New Testament, whereas today we tend to think of the soul more as the center of wisdom, goodness, and intuition in the body and less the source of life itself.

The soul is the subject of much of literature, particularly fantasy literature. Phillip Pullman's *His Dark Materials* trilogy is, in fact, obsessed with the notion of the soul, which Pullman calls a person's "dæmon" and which defines his or her very nature. In Pullman's trilogy, a soulless person is a ghost of his former self and either shows no emotion or dies, much like those in the wizarding world whose souls have been sucked out by a Dementor's Kiss (see Chapter 15). A person without a soul, or with only a portion of a soul, could be thought of as less than human, and in fact would become less so, the further removed he was, in time, from the other part of his soul.

This definition (less than human) befits Lord Voldemort, who created not one Horcrux, but six, thus splitting his soul into seven pieces. His Horcruxes include his diary; two family heirlooms (a ring and a locket); a cup that belonged to one of the Hogwarts founders, Helga Hufflepuff; and two others, yet unknown. (Voldemort's snake and companion, Nagini, is thought to be a possibility, but also likely is that the two remaining Horcruxes belonged to Hogwarts founders, much like Helga's cup. See Chapter 16 for the latest updates.)

Part 5

Regulating Magic and the Wizards Who Perform It

As with any community, wizards require a method of governing themselves, and the Ministry of Magic fills that role. In this part, you discover the similarities between British and wizard forms of government, take a visit to the Ministry itself, and find out what happens to wizards who break the rules. You also get a bonus chapter, which highlights the people, places, and wizarding tools found in Rowling's seventh and final novel in the series, *Harry Potter and the Deathly Hallows*.

Chapter 14

The Ministry of Magic

In This Chapter

+ Getting a glimpse at the old Wizards' Council

+ Reviewing the function of each of the seven Ministry departments

+ Discovering how wizards and British politicos liaise

Located deep underground in the center of London, the Ministry of Magic is the governing body for wizards (and for all creatures with magical abilities) in Great Britain, similar in many ways to British and American forms of federal government. However, as this chapter shows, several governmental functions that appear in both Great Britain and the United States simply don't exist in the Ministry's seven departments, and vice versa.

The (Now Defunct) Wizards' Council

Prior to the creation of the Ministry of Magic more than 400 years ago, UK wizards were governed by the Wizards' Council. The Council spent much of its early days defining Being and Beast, in order to determine who should participate in the Council, and who shouldn't.

MAGIC TALE

Wizards' Councils appear in two of the most influential fantasy book series: J.R.R. Tolkien's *The Lord of the Rings* and Ursula Le Guin's *Earthsea* series. In *Rings*, Gandalf is a member of the White Council, the fraternity of wizards of which Saruman the White (and, later, Gandalf the White himself) is head. In *Earthsea*, a mature Ged becomes Archmage, head of the wizards' council.

Ministry Departments Galore

Seven departments make up the Ministry of Magic, and they are described in the following sections.

Upon comparing the Ministry to both British and American federal governments, however, we find some startling omissions in the wizarding world:

+ *Exchequer/Treasury:* Wizards don't appear to pay taxes of any sort, yet Ministry officials do manage to get paid. Given that no governmental body can operate without funds, somewhere, buried deep in London, there must be an exchequer or treasury department at the Ministry. Perhaps we just don't know about it. Or maybe the Exchequer has an office in the Department of Mysteries (see the final section of this chapter).

+ *Work and Pensions/Labor and Social Security:* As with the lack of an Exchequer, the Ministry of Magic has no ministry or department that deals with labor and pension issues. However, jobs are hardly scarce in the wizarding world: careers with the Ministry, at Hogwarts, at St. Mungo's (see Chapter 7), at Gringotts (see Chapter 4), and in retail and service businesses do appear to be readily available, limited only by one's lack of distinction in various school subjects at Hogwarts. In addition, elderly, retired wizards give all appearances of being well cared for and able to manage their finances quite well. So perhaps the wizarding community is in the unique position of having enough jobs available for the people who want them, and having citizens who plan for retirement.

+ *Education:* Note that there is no Department of Education as there is in both UK and U.S. governments. Hogwarts, as the only British wizarding school, effectively functions as the education department of the Ministry. All decisions related to the training of wizards are made at Hogwarts and by Hogwarts staff. However, the Ministry of Magic has the power to adjust curriculum, change school rules with educational decrees, expel students from Hogwarts, and replace headmasters and/or professors who aren't up to snuff.

+ *Housing:* Nearly every government throughout the world has to deal, at some point, with lack of housing, overcrowded housing, unsafe urban dwellings, and/or unprofitable rural housing and farms. However, the Ministry of Magic does not appear to have any department or office that helps wizards locate affordable, appropriate housing for themselves and their families.

Those are the departments that do *not* exist in the Ministry. The following are the seven departments that *do* exist.

Department of Magical Games and Sports

The Department of Magical Games and Sports coordinates all international competitions held on British soil, and also regulates intra-British sports and games. The British and Irish Quidditch League Headquarters has an office under this department, as does the Official Gobstones Club (see Chapter 6 for more on Quidditch and Gobstones).

One unusual office in this department is the Ludicrous Patents Office. No one is quite sure whether the agency is actively *encouraging* ludicrous patents, or whether this office is sniffing out the ludicrous ones and throwing those patent applications away.

British government has a similar agency to the Department of Magical Games and Sports in the Department for Culture, Media and Sport, which oversees and coordinates with museums and galleries, libraries, architecture, historic building, and the like. This British department also funds public broadcasting, including the BBC, promotes British tourism, encourages creative industries, and sponsors sporting opportunities and events, from grade-school to elite levels.

KING'S ENGLISH

An elevator, called a lift in Great Britain, transports wizards and witches deep under London to the offices of the Ministry. The most dangerous departments are the farthest from the surface, which makes sense.

No such centralized department exists in American politics, although small offices and divisions oversee some similar entities. Sports and games are nearly all self-regulated by sport governing bodies, with little or no government intervention. Even the U.S. Olympic Committee is a nonprofit organization, not a government agency.

Department of Magical Transportation

Every good government has an agency that deals with moving people from place to place (Department for Transport in London; Department of Transportation in Washington, D.C.), and the Ministry of Magic is no different. Chapter 5 discusses the four major ways wizards travel from place to place, which four key offices in this department regulate: the Floo Network Authority, the Broom Regulatory Control, the Portkey Office, and the Apparition Test Center.

These four offices operate very much like those in the Muggle world, where Muggle governments undertake tasks like regulating car emissions, licensing automobile drivers and their cars, regulating the safety of planes and trains, and so on.

Department of International Magical Cooperation

Governments of large, developed countries could, perhaps, take a lesson from the wizarding world and create their own "departments of international cooperation." Instead, the United States has the departments of State (the chief agency of international diplomacy and cooperation), Commerce (for cooperating in trade), and Defense (for when nations aren't feeling so cooperative). Similar departments exist in Great Britain: Foreign Affairs; International Development; Trade and Industry; and Defence.

The offices in this department include those related both to international trade and international law, as well as the British seats in the International Confederation of Wizards. Like the United Nations, the International Confederation of Wizards oversees all magical ministries and councils worldwide. This group initiated the International Code

KING'S ENGLISH

You say "defence," I say "defense" .... A number of British government terminologies are spelled oh-so-slightly differently than their American counterparts. **Centre** is center, **organisation** is organization, **licence** is license, and **byelaw** is bylaw. Go figure.

of Wizarding Secrecy, which is the international law that drives nearly all other laws and rules within the wizarding world: that Muggles cannot know of the existence of wizards and witches. The leader of the International Confederation of Wizards is called the Supreme Mugwump (see more in Chapter 1).

Department for Regulation and Control of Magical Creatures

As both one of the most enjoyable *and* one of the most dangerous jobs in the Ministry, working for the Department for Regulation and Control of Magical Creatures is a career without equal in American and British politics. The U.S. Department of Agriculture comes closest, but you can't compare the inspection of cows—a primary function of the USDA—with the excitement of transporting a dragon, the gratification that comes from helping wizards rid their homes of garden gnomes and doxies, and the danger of hunting fire crab poachers. But it's all in a day's work for the employees of this department.

Department of Magical Accidents and Catastrophes

This department has two aims:

+ To attempt to mend and cure wizards who have been injured by magic, either because of their own, er, lack of skill or because of an attack by another wizard.

+ To modify the memories of Muggles who have inadvertently witnessed magical activities.

Those two goals are met in two ways:

1. *St. Mungo's Hospital for Magical Maladies and Injuries:* Hidden
    in London, this hospital treats everything from injuries due to
    exploding cauldrons to dragon pox to unliftable jinxes. The facil-
    ity also acts as a nursing home, where wizards who have been
    put under the Cruciatus Curse (see Chapter 12)—and, thus, have
    been tortured until they become insane—are kept comfortable
    until they die.

2. *The Accidental Magic Reversal Squad:* An agency of this department,
    the squad rushes to the scene of magic and attempts to correct
    the damage done, much like an emergency medical technician
    (EMT) and ambulance driver might do in the Muggle world. If no
    Muggles have seen the results of the accident, the wizard involved
    is treated and either taken to St. Mungo's or released, albeit with
    a hefty fine. But if Muggles *have* seen magic go awry, as is usually
    the case when unlicensed wizards attempt Apparition and leave
    body parts in two different places, or when Dark Wizards kill and
    maim indiscriminately, the memories of Muggles who survive the
    incident must be altered.

    Obliviators who work for the squad are expert at performing
    memory charms (see Chapter 12), thus removing any memory of
    the incident from the minds of the Muggles.

Muggles in the United States and United Kingdom do not have an
equivalent department: the British Department of Health and the U.S.
Department of Health and Human Services are involved in treating and
correcting maladies, but do not deal with cleaning up catastrophes.

Likewise, the U.S. Department of Homeland Security (with groups like
the Federal Emergency Management Agency) deals regularly with catastrophes, but would never attempt to change the public's perception of the
event. Wait a minute … maybe these two departments aren't so different
after all!

Department of Magical Law Enforcement

The Department of Magical Law Enforcement is structured nearly identically to the U.S. Justice Department and the British Home Office. But unlike United States and British law, law enforcement in the magical world (see Chapter 15) has only two priorities: avoiding Muggle detection and protecting wizards.

International Code of Wizarding Secrecy requires every wizarding government to take strenuous precautions to avoid detection from Muggles, resorting to the memory-altering tactics employed by the Department of Magical Accidents and Catastrophes, as needed. For this reason, offices within the Department of Magical Law Enforcement make it illegal for wizards to both improperly use magic and misuse Muggle artifacts. There is no equivalent agency that comes close in the Muggle world.

To keep powerful and/or Dark Wizards from taking advantage of other wizards, the Department of Magical Law Enforcement vigorously protects the wizards within its borders. For wizards engaging in fraudulent, but otherwise harmless, activities, the Office for Detection and Confiscation of Counterfeit Defensive Spells and Protective Objects (a mouthful!) prosecutes to the fullest extent of the law. For more evil deeds, the Magical Law Enforcement Patrol (or Squad) is on hand to make arrests, and Aurors (see Chapter 15) both track criminals and protect innocent citizens in danger. This service is much like the Federal Bureau of Investigation (United States) and the Serious Organised Crime Agency (UK).

To prosecute crimes, the Wizengamot Administration Services acts as the high court, like the United States Supreme Court. You can find more on the Wizengamot in Chapter 15.

Department of Mysteries   .

Aaaah, the Department of Mysteries. Very secret are the goings on of this government agency; so much so that those employed by this department are called Unspeakables. It's not that they *can't* speak, it's that they *don't*.

An equivalent agency in British and American government probably exists, but who knows, really? Governments are full of mysterious activities; few advertise the fact by actively naming a department of "mysteries." Remember that the U.S. government was able to develop and test atomic bombs in complete secrecy during World War II's Manhattan Project in Oak Ridge, Tennessee. Residents of that "Secret City" were not allowed to speak to anyone outside the town limits about what they were working on ... the Unspeakables of the Muggle world. Similarly, the Central Intelligence Agency (United States) and Secret Intelligence Service (UK) are responsible for all foreign espionage, and those employed at those agencies are not allowed to speak to outsiders about their jobs. Perhaps there's even a link between Rowling's Unspeakables and the so-called "Untouchables," government officials who went after mobster Al Capone in the 1920s.

The Link Between British Government and the Ministry of Magic

According to Rowling, upon the election of each new British Prime Minister, the Minister of Magic must contact the Muggle Prime Minister (through a portrait of a wizard hanging on the Prime Minister's wall) to meet and discuss the existence of wizards, magic, and the Ministry of Magic itself. The Minister of Magic must also inform the Prime Minister whenever highly dangerous creatures are brought into the country or when Dark Wizards threaten the security of Muggles in general or the Prime Minister directly. Aurors have even been known to infiltrate the Prime Minister's staff in order to guard and protect him under this last set of conditions.

What's fascinating about this idea is that it forces readers to wonder, "Do wizards really exist in England, and the Prime Minister just doesn't want to admit it?" It helps explain how the wizarding world has survived, undetected, all these millennia. In fact, one could argue that Rowling's particular genius comes not only from creating an entire fantastical world, but in joining that world with the Muggle world and explaining ways in which the two have been intersecting for years. That concept gives readers pause, even those older, worldly, experienced readers. Is it possible? Did the Minister of Magic introduce himself through a picture in the wall to Margaret Thatcher back in the 1980s? What about Tony Blair more recently?

Each Muggle Prime Minister, of course, tells no one what he or she knows and takes the knowledge of magic and wizards to the grave. Why? Because if the Prime Minister passed along his knowledge of the Ministry of Magic and the entire wizarding world, his mental state would quite surely be questioned, and he would likely find himself turned out of 10 Downing Street in a half-day's time.

TOURIST TIP

If you plan to make a trip to 10 Downing, you might get close enough to snap a picture of the sign that reads, "Downing Street" at the end of the block, or possibly even catch a glimpse of the Prime Minister as he gets into his Land Rover limousine. Forget getting any closer than that, as security is as tight as at the White House.

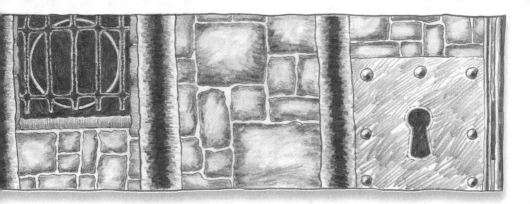

Chapter 15

Crime and Punishment

In This Chapter

+ Understanding the role of the Ministry

+ Getting to know Aurors

+ Examining the wizard court: the Wizengamot

+ Reviewing wizard forms of punishment, including Azkaban prison

As with all societies, rules and laws exist to govern the wizarding world. Among British wizards, laws are established by the Ministry of Magic, and they are enforced by Ministry department officials, Aurors, and the Wizengamot. Convicted criminals are punished, but punishments tend to be light for pranks gone wrong and for crimes committed out of monetary greed. For the use of Dark Magic, however, punishment is fierce: a term at a prison from which there is little chance of escape.

Ministry Department Officials: Tracking Down the Improper Use of Magic

Improper use of magic—the misdemeanors of the wizarding world—includes any of the following:

+ *Playing pranks on Muggles:* Because Muggles cannot defend themselves against magic of any sort, playing pranks on nonmagic folk is strictly forbidden. Wizards sometimes enjoy playing pranks on Muggles by magicking up their toilets, doorknobs, cars, and so on. Is there an equivalent in the Muggle world? Not exactly. This is something like an eighth-grader picking on a kindergartener, which may be a school violation but isn't a crime. Perhaps white-color crime comes the closet—when those with more power pick on those with less.

+ *Using standard Muggle items in magical ways:* Items commonly used by Muggles (and that, incidentally, are generally useless to wizards) are not allowed to be doctored up by magic. No similar "crime" exists in the Muggle world, although Muggles frequently *use* items in ways they weren't originally intended. It's just not considered a crime in the Muggle world.

+ *Allowing Muggles to see magic being performed:* Because Muggles are not supposed to know that wizards exist, the Statute of Secrecy strictly forbids allowing Muggles to see magical acts being performed. Muggles' memories are always modified by Ministry officials (called Obliviators) when they see such acts. In the Muggle world, the United States CIA reportedly has its own way of "wiping out someone's memory" if they've seen something they shouldn't have ... yikes!

Note that, as in most cultures, wizard self-defense is always permitted, which means that in exceptional circumstances in which anyone's life is threatened, using magic in the presence of Muggles is allowed.

+ *Misusing magical creatures:* Because so many magical creatures are dangerous, possessing and misusing such creatures is a crime under wizard law. Cruelty to animals, the equivalent crime in the Muggle world, does sometimes go unpunished in local courts, even though studies show that it's a precursor to more serious crimes.

+ *Cheating other wizards:* Cheating other wizards can range from selling useless amulets and substandard cauldrons to outright theft. In the wizarding world, as in nearly all Muggle societies, cheating others is strictly forbidden.

Thus, Ministry department officials act as a police force for petty crimes (what we might call misdemeanors). For crimes committed out of sheer evil—and especially for the use of the Unforgivable Curses (see Chapter 12)—Aurors hunt down the wizards in question, and the Wizengamot prosecutes the offenders, usually with a life-long term in prison.

When the only person hurt from the misuse of magic is the wizard him- or herself (such as is the case with many injuries), and no Muggles have seen the results of the misused magic, no one is punished. The injury is treated, the wizard may be publicly embarrassed, and he or she usually has to pay a fine, but the wizard is usually not prosecuted. This is generally the same as in the Muggle world, where if there is no one to press charges against an individual, and no damage was done to someone else's property (including community-owned property), the individual is sent home, perhaps with a ticket or light fine.

Ridding the World of Evil Magic: Aurors, the Wizengamot, and Anti-Dark Wizard Groups

While Ministry department officials detect and deter petty crimes, Aurors are homicide detectives, the FBI, and the CIA all rolled into one, and the Wizengamot hears cases brought to trial by the work of Aurors. In addition, other wizards sometimes come together to fight Dark Magic.

Aurors and Their Role

Aurors are employed by the Ministry as part of the Magical Law Enforcement Squad, are sometimes called Hit Wizards, and are the top police force in the British wizarding world. These law-enforcement wizards likely take their name from *aurora*, Latin for dawn or daybreak. (Aurora was, in fact, the name of the Roman goddess of the dawn.) As defenders against Dark Wizards, Aurors are wizards of light.

KING'S ENGLISH

A common story about the origin of the word **Auror** is that, because British police officers are colloquially known as "coppers," Rowling named the Auror after the Latin *aurum* or *aureum*, meaning "gold." This is a bit of a stretch, though. If this sort of thin connection were Rowling's style, it could be equally likely that Aurors were named after the Latin *auris*, meaning ear or hearing, because they listened well enough in class to earn top marks! Pretty unlikely.

Aurors are among the most accomplished wizards in the world, excelling in several school subjects, including Defense Against the Dark Arts, Transfiguration, Potions, and Charms. Animagi and Metamorphmagi (discussed in detail in Chapter 13) are prime candidates for Auror work, because they can easily change their appearance. Aurors must also be of outstanding character, because they are deeply entrenched in the Dark world and cannot be at risk of changing sides. Before taking their posts, Aurors train for three years beyond graduation from Hogwarts.

Think of qualifying to be an Auror the same way you might think of getting accepted to one of the U.S. military academies (West Point, the Navel Academy, and the Air Force Academy), which require a successful candidate to be an exceptional student *and* an exceptional role model. Applicants to the academies must receive recommendations from members of Congress to submit with their applications! Once there, the rigors of the academies are radically different from life at other colleges—course loads are heavier, nearly every student follows a basic engineering curriculum, military and physical training is required, and so on.

The Order of the Phoenix

In addition to Aurors, nonofficial anti-Dark Wizard groups occasionally spring up in the wizarding world. The most potent is the Order of the Phoenix, which is made up of powerful wizards and Aurors alike, yet meets secretly, outside of the Ministry's purview. This group is, in fact, in opposition to the Ministry, during those times that the ministry is in denial over the existence of Dark Wizards. Like orders of knights throughout British history, who upheld the laws of the land even when kings had gone bad, the Order upholds the laws of the Ministry when the Ministry is too blinded or corrupt to take on that task itself. The Order's symbol, a phoenix, is a colorful bird that lives for hundreds of years, periodically bursting into flame and renewing itself with new plumage and life (see Chapter 2).

Prosecuting Dark Wizards: The Wizengamot

The Wizengamot is the Wizard High Court and is made up of the best and brightest wizards of the day. The Wizengamot has similarities to both the United States Supreme Court and the UK House of Lords (a legislative body much like the United States Senate, whose judicial functions will be replaced by a UK Supreme Court in 2008), as both are the highest court in the land. However, both the U.S. and UK versions are appeals courts, in that they hear only cases that have been heard in lower courts. The Wizengamot, on the other hand, hears new cases, almost always criminal trials for crimes in which Dark Magic was used.

When they sit in full session, the fifty or so members of the Wizengamot are presided over by a Chief Warlock. Likewise, a Chief Justice presides over the nine justices on the United States Supreme Court, and a Senior heads the twelve UK law lords (although only five of those twelve usually sit at trial). Of the two, however, the Wizengamot is much more like the United States Supreme Court: members wear robes, proceed formally, may block the public from attending trials, and so on. (By contrast, the House of Lords' proceedings are quite informal.) The Wizengamot Charter of Rights, a listing of basic wizard rights, sounds strikingly like the Bill of Rights that were amended to the U.S. Constitution, the document upon which the United States Supreme Court bases all its decisions.

However, unlike the United States Supreme Court, members of the Wizengamot act as prosecutors and interrogators during trials and may even skip the part where they hear evidence on behalf of the defendant. At times when the Chief Warlock has not been a person with a well-defined sense of justice, the Wizengamot have come to the court with their minds made up, and cases have been based on hearsay, with no witnesses or assistance for the defense. (This is frighteningly like the trials in some non-democratic countries around the world today.) As a result, defendants and witnesses appearing before the Wizengamot can be so nervous that they do not insist on the unbiased proceedings that are their right; in fact, rights under the Charter may be ignored by the Wizengamot. Indeed, at some proceedings, the charge is read, and then a vote (a show of hands) is taken to determine guilt or innocence; no other trial proceedings take place. And in extreme cases, no trial at all takes place; the accused is sent straight to Azkaban. This is not a legally sanctioned practice; it's just what happens when the Ministry panics.

Magic Tale

Proceedings of the Wizengamot court sometimes sound an awful lot like the Salem Witch Trials. With no means of defense against charges, wizards may be found guilty of practicing Dark Magic, even though no trial is heard and no defense is argued on behalf of the accused. The assumption is that if Aurors went after and captured a wizard, he or she must be a Dark Wizard. But situations can be confused, and good wizards have been wrongly imprisoned in Azkaban, just as innocent people were tortured or killed by hasty court proceedings in Salem, Massachusetts.

The Wizengamot has repeatedly sent Dark Wizards to prison, which is essentially a death sentence. The Wizengamot can also dole out lesser punishments, but only rarely hears cases that do not involve Dark Magic. As with Muggle courts of law, accused criminals can exchange testimony on other criminals for lighter sentences.

The name Wizengamot likely has a double meaning, both that of being made up of wise wizards and being made up of *old* wizards. *Gamut* means "entire range," (and in Tagalog, the largest of the Philippine languages, *gamot* means "medicine") while *wizen* means "dried up and shriveled." A range of dried up and shriveled people? The medicine of the dried and shriveled? Hmmm. Perhaps, but *wizen* is likely derived from *wizard*, which means "wise." The Wizengamot, then, can be thought of as made up of a range of wise, albeit a bit old, people. Or the medicine of old, wise wizards … tough medicine to swallow, for those found guilty.

Punishments

In nearly all democratic societies, punishment has four purposes:

+ *Retribution:* This purpose of punishment appears in the Old Testament "eye for an eye," and is often referred to as "paying a debt to society." This debt is usually tied to the heinousness of the crime: a lesser crime receives a lesser punishment.

+ *Deterrence:* Punishment is meant to deter others from committing the same crime and to keep a criminal from repeating the crime in the future. The punishment must, therefore, be severe enough to act as a deterrent.

+ *Rehabilitation:* Ideally, punishment also includes a component that rehabilitates the criminal, eliminating the underlying cause of criminal activity (mental illness, extreme anger, drug use, and so on).

+ *Incapacitation:* Punishment is meant to restrain the criminal in order to keep him or her from committing additional criminal acts. Incapacitation ranges from house arrest to death.

In the wizarding world, retribution and rehabilitation tend to be ignored; the focus is, instead, on deterrence and incapacitation. Underage criminals are deterred by the risk of expulsion from school, and adult criminals are deterred by the risk of fines and public humiliation. Evil criminals are supposed to be deterred and incapacitated by sentences in Azkaban prison, but the most evil ones tend to break out and continue their criminal ways.

Expulsion

The Ministry of Magic has no power to punish Hogwarts students for the crimes they commit at school, nor does it have the power to expel students from Hogwarts. However, the Hogwarts headmaster does have that power, and he uses it as a chief deterrent to underage mischief.

Wizards-in-training are not allowed, for all practical purposes, to practice magic outside school grounds. However, this violation tends to be prosecuted by school officials only when it allows Muggles to see magic being performed or when it employs the use of Dark Magic. Playing Quidditch (see Chapter 6) in the backyard, for example, with no Muggle neighbors nearby, would not result in expulsion. Messing with helpless Muggles on the subway, on the other hand, would. This legal turning of the head happens all the time in the Muggle world ... think of a police car sailing past cars going well over the speed limit on some major highways, for example!

Like Muggle high schools, although wizarding students do drop out of Hogwarts before completing their seven years, most wizarding jobs require education through at least the fifth year (when O.W.L.s are taken—see Chapter 8) or the sixth (when Apparition lessons are offered—see Chapter 5), so incentive is high for students to remain at Hogwarts until at least that time.

Wizards are considered to be "of age" when they turn seventeen, which is either late in their sixth year or early in their seventh. (In the Muggle world, it's usually sixteen to drop out of school; eighteen to be considered a legal adult. The wizarding world does both at seventeen.) As such, seventh-year students cannot be expelled from Hogwarts for underage sorcery, as they are no longer considered underage. They could, possibly, be expelled for being gits and prats, though!

KING'S ENGLISH

A **git** roughly translates to "jerk," but with a touch of jealousy to it and with a little bit of love. So your best friend is a git when she wins the spelling bee, and then forgets your birthday the next day. The boys at Hogwarts often call each other gits. A **prat** is an idiot, but at Hogwarts it also tends to be an uptight idiot: one who doesn't quite get what's going on, but is trying to be perfect anyway. Percy Weasley is a perfect example of a goody-two-shoes prat who has little common sense.

Fines and Public Humiliation

For the most part, wizards are kept in line for their minor crimes by small fines and public humiliation, if they can be caught. Repeat offenders of minor crimes are viewed with annoyance, and most are simply yelled at when they make their next public appearances. This sort of public embarrassment has recently been employed in the Muggle world, as when judges sentence bad teen drivers to several months of riding the bus, or sentence litterbugs to clean up the highway.

Azkaban Prison and Dementors

On the far other side of the spectrum from fines and humiliation is the deadly serious punishment of a sentence at Azkaban prison. In fact, the very name Azkaban strikes fear into the hearts of wizards. It is a place from which few wizards return, and when they do, they are often just a shell of their former selves.

Azkaban is much like the U.S. federal prison called Alcatraz (nicknamed "the Rock") that operated from the mid 1930s through the mid 1960s, both in name (three-syllable words beginning with the letter "a") and in location, as they are both island prisons. Both are maximum-security prisons that house the most dangerous criminals: in the case of Alcatraz, the most deadly mobsters and other murderers; in the case of Azkaban, the most evil Dark Wizards. Alcatraz has had only one successful escape attempt; Azkaban has had several.

TOURIST TIP

If you're visiting San Francisco, take the boat trip to Alcatraz Island to visit the prison, which is now a prime tourist destination and part of the Golden Gate National Recreation Area. Visit www.nps.gov/Alcatraz for more information.

The major difference between the two prisons, however, is the presence of dementors at Azkaban. Dementors (from the Latin *de*, out of, and *mens*, mind; or "to make insane") are Azkaban's prison guards: ghoulish, cloaked creatures (think of the Grim Reaper) who, just by being in the general vicinity of wizards and Muggles alike, suck happiness, peace, and hope right out of them. Victims in the presence of dementors feel a deep, whole-body coldness and remember painful events from the past. Because of the presence of these guards, many prisoners go mad in just a short time. In addition, for those requiring more serious punishment, they administer the Dementor's Kiss; dementors actually suck out the person's soul, so that he or she is nothing more than a walking shell. Most wizards die soon after the Dementor's Kiss. Compare this to even the meanest guards at Muggle prisons, and there's really no comparison.

Dementors can be kept at bay by conjuring up a Patronus (see Chapter 13), which acts as a positive force that shields the wizard from the soul-draining effects of the dementor. However, because the Patronus Charm is advanced wizardry, only the most accomplished wizards possess the ability to drive away the dementors. Happily, if one has been in the presence of a dementor and escapes, the ill effects can be quickly reversed by eating copious amounts of chocolate. Just one bite spreads warmth throughout the body and begins to bring joy back to the wizard. This is not unlike the role of chocolate in the Muggle world!

Rowling's depiction of dementors may have been influenced by the work of Philip Pullman, a British fantasy author. Rowling's dementors bear a striking resemblance to Pullman's Spectres in *His Dark Materials: The Subtle Knife*, published in 1997, two years before dementors first appeared in the wizarding world.

The word spectre, by definition, means any object of fear or dread, but Pullman's Spectres are especially dreaded. Although they cannot harm children, Spectres move toward adults as would a host of insects, and then they eat out the person's soul, leaving a mere shell of the person behind. Children can only watch this slow, soul-sucking death happening to their parents, older siblings, and other loved ones; they cannot stop the attacks or help defend against them. And children know that, in time, they, too, will be subject to Spectre attacks. The only defense against Spectres is the Subtle Knife, which can be borne only by the designated Knife Bearer.

Chapter 16

The Final Word

In This Chapter

+ Finding out who's good—and who's not

+ Getting the lowdown on a new gadget or two

+ Discovering a multitude of new incantations and spells

+ Learning more about Horcruxes

+ Latching on to additional advanced wizardry

This is the chapter in which you get the "final word" on the *Harry Potter* series. The seventh and final novel, *Harry Potter and the Deathly Hallows*, tied up a decade of loose ends, allowing fans to rest easy, knowing that good has prevailed and—at long last—Lord Voldemort has been vanquished.

In this chapter, you discover spells that appear for the first time in the last novel, get the latest on those horrible Horcruxes, and find out about the Deathly Hallows.

Good or Evil Revealed

So many questions about the goodness or badness of wizards lingered in the air before *Deathly Hallows* was published! Some cars even sported bumper stickers predicting that Snape was evil, while others begged for him to be trusted. When it was all said and done, audiences around the world were pleased to discover that Professor Snape is a good guy, loyal to the Order of the Phoenix to the end. Likewise, Mr. Ollivander, the wand-maker discussed in Chapter 7, is not a Dark Wizard, but was needed by Lord Voldemort for his knowledge of the Elder Wand (see "The Deathly Hallows" section later in this chapter). And the famed R. A. B. who stole a Horcrux from Voldemort (see both Chapter 13 and the "Horcruxes" section later in this chapter) was none other than Regulus Arcturus Black.

But perhaps the most intriguing character of the seventh novel is that of Ignotus Peverell, the original owner of the Invisibility Cloak (see Chapter 3), and an ancestor of Harry Potter. The surname *Peverell* belongs to an influential British family, and two English towns (Sampford Peverell and Bradford Peverell) bear the name. *Ignotus* is Latin for "unknown," which is an interesting choice for the bearer of the Invisibility Cloak.

Tourist Tip

If you want to taste the best vol-au-vent, a French pastry mentioned in *Deathly Hallows*, go to France, where you'll find them filled with escargot (snails) and other delicacies! Or, if you can't go to France, at least go to a French restaurant in New Orleans. Invented by Antonin Carême, an early-twentieth-century French pastry chef, vol-au-vent is a difficult pastry to create, because it's supposed to be extremely light and delicate. In fact, its name translates to "flight of the wind."

The Peverell family, along with many other wizarding families, lived in Godric's Hollow, an area named after Godric Gryffindor, one of the Hogwarts co-founders. This naming convention—a person's name, followed by the word "hollow"—is not only a British one. Deep in the Appalachian mountains (and in other rural, mountainous regions of the United States), streets and areas are named in this same way: "Xxx Hollow." Hollow is simply another word for "valley," and the family or person who settled a particular valley became its namesake.

A Healing Herb

Essence of Dittany is a wizarding cure-all that stops a wound from bleeding and quickly begins the healing process. Dittany also exists in the Muggle world, but it grows only in Crete, where its essential oil has long been prized by healers for digestive and rheumatic ailments. The plant itself is an herb that is supposed to have aphrodisiac properties, in addition to its ability to heal. The botanical name for White Dittany is *Dictamnus albus*—that's right, as in Albus Dumbledore—because *albus* is Latin for white.

New Incantations and Spells

Deathly Hallows brings a variety of new incantations and spells, many of which are used to protect homes and other areas.

As Lord Voldemort takes power over the wizarding world, more and more wizards must find ways to hide and protect themselves. In *Deathly Hallows*, Rowling gives us a variety of protective enchantments, including the following:

+ *Caterwauling Charm:* This unusual charm (with an unknown incantation) alerts Death Eaters when someone is moving about in Hogsmeade after dark. To "caterwaul" is to make a loud howling noise, a term derived from the Dutch word *kater*, for tomcat, an animal that makes a loud screeching sound when prowling for female cats.

+ *Cave Inimicum!:* This incantation has nothing to do with protecting a cave, which one might expect. Instead, it's derived from (no surprise!) Latin words (*cave* in this case is pronounced CAH-vay). From the Latin *caveo*, meaning guard against, beware of, or get security against, and *inimicum*, meaning hostile, harmful, enemy, or foe, this incantation guards against enemies.

+ *Muffliato!:* This protective enchantment (first introduced in *Half-Blood Prince*, but not used extensively until *Deathly Hallows*), derives from an old use of the word "muffle," in which a person's head and face were wrapped up (in a muff—that is, soft fur or other material) to keep the person from seeing or speaking. The person's voice—as well as any sound trying to reach the wrapped person's ears—were, therefore, muffled. Likewise, this incantation muffles conversations so that others cannot overhear them.

MAGIC TALE

On *Potterwatch*, an underground wizarding wireless program akin to the "Voice of America" during the Cold War, Remus Lupin uses the code name Romulus. Why? Because Remus and Romulus were brothers who reportedly became the founders of Rome. The boys were raised by a wolf and are the most famous of all feral children. Although Romulus later killed Remus, their connection to each other—and to wolves—is unmistakable.

+ *Protego Totalum!*: This incantation is an extension of the Shield Charm (which has the incantation *Protego!*—see Chapter 12), adding the Latin *totum*, which means entire or the whole of. Therefore, this charm shields, well, everything!

+ *Repello Muggletum!*: This incantation is derived from the Latin *repello*, meaning drive back or repulse, the made-up word Muggle (referring to people without wizarding powers), and the Latin *tum*, meaning at the moment. In other words, repulse Muggles now!

+ *Salvio Hexia!*: From the Latin *salvus*, meaning safe and undamaged, this is a general safety hex.

+ *The Taboo:* This curse is one of Rowling's most creative, because it jinxes Voldemort's name so that anyone using it immediately loses all of the previously mentioned protective enchantments. Of course, Harry Potter is one of the few wizards who ever uses Voldemort's name (instead of calling him "You-Know-Who" or "He-Who-Must-Not-Be-Named"), so this curse is an ingenious way for Voldemort to quickly find Harry. By definition, a *taboo* is a Polynesian word that refers to a sacred curse put on a person or object, rendering him (or her or it) untouchable or even unmentionable. Thus, Voldemort's name becomes unmentionable; but when it is mentioned, it enacts a curse.

KING'S ENGLISH

A **kissing gate**, like the one placed at the entrance to the Godric's Hollow cemetery, is an entirely British concept—a gate that can't accidentally be left open. One half of the gate swings back and forth, like any gate would. But the other half traps the swing side with two parallel walls of fencing. The swing side is stopped in one direction by one wall, and in the other direction by the other wall, so that it can swing only a few feet in either direction. One person at a time can pass through the gate by slithering sideways between the swing gate and either wall, but most farm animals can't figure it out! This type of gate is common at the entrance to a graveyard, because it effectively keeps farm animals from wandering in and grazing on the cemetery grass.

Rowling introduces many more spells in *Deathly Hallows*, above and beyond the protective enchantments:

+ *Confringo! (Blasting Curse)*: From the Latin *confringo*, meaning to break into pieces, this curse explodes just about anything, including an entire room.

+ *Defodio!*: From the Latin *defodio*, meaning dig or bury, this incantation enlarges a passageway, blasting it apart, if necessary.

+ *Deprimo!*: From the Latin *deprimo*, meaning to sink or keep down, this incantation blasts a hole into whatever is below you and lowers you quickly. This incantation is like *Descendo!*

+ *Descendo!*: From the Latin *descendo*, meaning to descend or fall, this incantation causes something to lower.

+ *Duro!*: This rather frightening incantation turns cloth into stone—and may, in fact, turn anything into stone. Turning objects into stone has a long history in fairy tales, especially those involving trolls, and both Lewis's *The Lion, the Witch and the Wardrobe* and Tolkien's *The Lord of the Rings* include stone-turning. This spell is taken straight from the Latin *duro*, which means to make something hard, like steel.

+ *Geminio! (Gemino Curse)*: This curse makes many copies of an object—so many, in fact, that you might literally be squished to death if this happens in a small room. From the Latin *gemino*, meaning to double the force of, or repeat.

✦ *Glisseo!:* This ultra-fun incantation turns stairs into a slide or chute. From the French *glissade*, this is a ballet term that means glide or slide. It's derived from *glisser*, an Old French word meaning to glide, which has the same root as the word "glacier."

✦ *Homenum revelio!:* From the Latin *homo*, meaning human being, and *revelo*, meaning reveal, it's not a big surprise that this incantation tells the wizard whether a human is present. The Latin *ad hominem* literally means "argument against the man" and is a way of replaying to an argument or claim by attacking the person. This approach is today known as an *ad hominem* attack.

✦ *Obscuro!:* Pulled directly from the Latin *obscuro*, meaning to conceal, obscure, or darken, this incantation puts a blindfold over someone's eyes.

✦ *Piertotum Locomotor!:* From the Latin *pietas*, meaning loyalty and dutifulness, and *totum*, meaning all of or entire, this intriguing incantation makes statues and suits of armor come to life and protect Hogwarts. Evoking this incantation means, "All you loyal ones, *move!*"

✦ *Protego Horribilis!:* From the Latin *protego*, meaning to protect or defend, and *horribilis*, meaning terrible, horrible, or monstrous, this incantation is used to guard Hogwarts against impending attackers (at least attackers who are terrible, horrible, and monstrous, which, let's face it, most are).

✦ *The Trace:* This charm finally reveals how underage wizarding activity is detected by Ministry officials. The English word trace is derived from the Latin *tractus*, which means dragging or pulling along. This is interesting, because that's exactly what the Trace is doing: dragging or pulling along evidence of underage wizardry. The name also resonates with watchers of TV crime shows, who know that investigators always look for traces of the criminal—any mark or evidence left at the scene of the crime.

Horcruxes

Horcruxes are central to Rowling's sixth and seventh novels, and you can find the basics on these evil containers in Chapter 13. But new information tells us that each Horcrux is strikingly similar to the Ring of Power in Tolkien's *The Lord of the Rings*. Like the One Ring, a Horcrux worn around one's neck gradually weighs down the wearer, making him or her more and more fatigued. But as with the Ring, the fatigue is far more than physical, because both the One Ring and a Horcrux can make those people around the object think the worst of others. These evil magical objects play on internal fears, causing anyone close to them to begin to doubt others—and themselves.

Rowling tells us that people can get emotionally attached to Horcruxes; in fact, a portion of a soul stored inside the Horcrux can get *into* someone so attached. This has echoes of Tolkien's Gollum, who became so emotionally attached to the Ring that he thought of it as a person, his Precious. Perhaps the Ring contained a portion of the soul of Sauron (who is otherwise bodyless). The similarities are eerie.

We also find out that Horcruxes cannot be summoned through a Summoning Spell, nor can they be destroyed by any but the most magical of objects (just as the Ring cannot be destroyed by anything but the fires of Mount Doom). And we discover the identity of the final two Horcruxes: the diadem (which is like a small crown) of Rowena Ravenclaw (a Hogwarts founder), and Nagini, Voldemort's snake.

But perhaps the most important new information about Horcruxes comes in the form of Rowling's spiritual admonition: that to undo a Horcrux (to unsplit your soul), you must feel great remorse, and in doing so, the pain of that remorse can kill you. Anyone who has ever done any-thing hurtful or regretful can tap into that idea!

The Deathly Hallows

The Deathly Hallows aren't so much advanced wizardry as they are components of a wizarding fairy tale that turn out to be true! Wizard children are raised on fairy tales just as Muggle children are, although the titles and the content differ. But a cornerstone of wizarding fairy tales is the story of the three Peverell brothers who possessed the Deathly Hallows.

> ### Tourist Tip
>
> The Forest of Dean, an important setting in *Deathly Hallows*, is a real place in Gloucestershire County, England. Originally settled by the Romans, it was later the royal hunting grounds of the Tudor kings. Today, it ranks as the most family-friendly tourist attraction in England. If you're in London and want to check it out, visit www.visitforestofdean.co.uk.

The word *hallow* is drawn from Old English and German terms that all mean something holy or sacred. Thus, the Deathly Hallows refer to sacred items that are related to death in some way. There are three Hallows:

+ *The Elder Wand* (its symbol is a line): This special wand, one that is supposed to vanquish all other wands, is called both the Deathstick and the Wand of Destiny; that is, it can either be used for evil or for good. But like Tolkien's Ring of Power, it's awfully tough to wield something that powerful and use it only for good.

  "Elder" is an interesting name for this wand, because that word has several meanings and interpretations. In the most well-known sense of the word, it means oldest or even ancient, as the wand likely is. Elder also means highest-ranking or of superior rank, like elders in a church, marking the wand as the single most powerful wand in the world. Elder also refers to a small tree that's best known for its jam-friendly berries (elderberries), so the name could allude to the wood used to make it. Finally, the Elder Futhark is a Germanic and Norse runic alphabet, the oldest of such alphabets (see Chapter 13 for more on runes). Elder Futhark runes were inscribed on weapons (and the wand is quite a weapon!) for hundreds of years; in fact, the angular shape of the runic alphabet is thought to exist because of the constraints of metal- and wood-stamping the second through eighth centuries, angles being far easier to stamp than rounded markings. Thus the name could refer to any runic markings that may exist on the wand itself.

+ *The Resurrection Stone* (its symbol is a circle): This stone is not another Sorcerer's Stone, but instead enables ghostly renditions of the dead not to actually come back to life, but to interact with the stone-bearer. This can be detrimental if the stone-bearer chooses to focus too much on the shades of the dead and fails to live himself.

In July 1981 (when J.K. Rowling would have been in her teens), *The Avengers* comic book featured an episode called "The Resurrection Stone." This stone is strikingly similar to Rowling's stone, in that it could bring the dead back to life, although it was more powerful than Rowling's stone, because it didn't just bring back a spirit, but brought back the body, the spirit—the whole enchilada. Questers in *The Avengers* story sought this stone, just as wizards do. But the comic-book stone was deeply evil—as with a Horcrux, something within the stone communicated with anyone holding it, temping them in various malevolent ways. We know that Rowling's Stone has the power to badly damage any human trying to use it, but it is not necessarily evil.

+ *The Cloak of Invisibility* (its symbol is a triangle): This cloak is the Invisibility Cloak discussed in Chapter 3, and it may seem rather benign compared to the other Hallows. But as Bilbo discovered when wearing the Ring of Power in Tolkien's *The Hobbit*, being invisible can be incredibly powerful, even when one does still have a corporeal body and leaves footprints!

The Deathly Hallows are a little like the Rock, Paper, Scissors children's game, in that each can both beat and be beaten by the others. The Hallows, however, moved beyond children's stories or games and into a true quest for the three objects for many wizards, who believed that any person who bore all three Hallows would be unbeatable. Likewise, those seeking the Stone in *The Avengers* and those seeking the Ring (which, like the cloak, made the wearer invisible) in *The Lord of the Rings* also believed that owning such objects would make them all-powerful for eternity. Such was the case for the wizard called Grindelwald (see Chapter 1), who believed the Hallows actually existed and sought them, hoping to do good with them, but growing increasingly evil until he was the epitome of wizard Darkness. Dumbledore defeated Grindelwald in 1945.

Rowling also makes a commentary on children's literature in her explanation of the Hallows, telling her readers that children's fairy tales might just have more power in them than we think. Lord Voldemort, it turns out, has no respect for children's stories (the fiend!), so he does not believe the stories of the Hallows and thus misses his chance to be unbeatable.

Fiendfyre

Fiendfyre is cursed fire—that is, a powerful brand of Dark Magic that creates fire-breathing monsters that can consume buildings, people, and even Horcruxes. The word *fiend* is derived from a couple of Old English terms that mean hate, which points to the Dark nature of fiendfyre. "The Fiend" is also a term that means Satan, so we see again that the term *fiend* refers to deep evil. Fyre, on the other hand, is the Middle English spelling of "fire" that we see in *Beowulf*, for example. Originally from the German *pyre*, meaning golden embers, the word gradually changed to *fyre*, and finally, *fire*.

MAGIC TALE

Besom, which is used as a term of degradation in *Deathly Hallows* ("you old besom"), doesn't mean biddy or hag or scoundrel, as you may think. Instead, it means a broom—specifically, a bundle of twigs tied to a handle (which exactly describes the brooms of the wizarding world). Celtic witches have long been reported to use besoms to clean and purify their sacred spaces—kind of a feng shui thing. Incidentally, the broom used in the sport of curling is also called a besom.

The Journey Ends

And so the journey of Harry Potter, Ron, Hermione, Dumbledore, Snape, Voldemort, and all the others in Rowling's cast of characters comes to a close. For more than 4,000 pages that were more than 10 years in the making, Rowling has kept readers delighted, intrigued, and even at times frightened (case in point: the first chapter of *Goblet of Fire*).

Rowling excels as a writer of scenes, which means that for over 90 percent of those pages, Harry and company are walking, eating, talking—this is, moving and acting in some way. Rowling also creates characters that are impossible not to love (or hate, as the case may be), such that readers celebrate each victory and grieve each setback—and there were so many of those. But mostly, Rowling's gift for detail is what sets her apart; she never misses an opportunity to describe the magical world with such specificity that ... well, that we believe it actually exists. What Harry Potter fan hasn't wanted to yell *Accio keys!* when running late, hasn't wanted to Apparate or use a Portkey (or bewitch a car to fly) to avoid rush hour traffic, or hasn't wished a love potion or truth serum actually exists. It's a world we all fantasize about living in—sans an evil Dark Lord and corrupt government, of course. But even that intrigues us, because we hope we would all be as brave, noble, and humble as Harry and his friends, should such evil overtake the world.

Appendix A

Glossary of British Terms

Great Britain and the United States are as much alike as two countries on different continents could be. But in spite of the similarities, some British terminology may have you scratching your head. This appendix helps you understand British terms that appear in the *Harry Potter* novels.

balaclava   Ski mask.

ball   A dance similar to an American prom.

bang on course   On target.

bang out of order   Out of line.

bangers   Large sausages served as part of an afternoon or evening meal, usually with mashed potatoes.

bangers and mash   Sausages and mashed potatoes.

bin   Trash can.

biscuit   A cookie, usually bought and served in a tin (a round metal box with a lid); also a cracker that's something like an American saltine, but more dense and often served with cheese.

blancmange   A type of pudding.

blimey   Golly; geez.

bloke   Fellow; guy.

boater   Flat straw hat.

bogey   Booger; snot.

bonbons   Round treats that usually have a slightly crusty outside and a chewy center, coated in powdered sugar.

bowler hat   A formal black hat with a narrow brim.

brewpub   A pub in which beer is brewed onsite.

brilliant   Excellent; incredible.

budgerigar   A type of parakeet.

camp bed   Fold-up cot.

carriage   Train car.

cheek, giving   Being a smart-mouth.

chipolatas   Small pork sausages usually served at breakfast; what Americans might call "breakfast sausage" or even "cocktail sausage."

chocolate gateau   A rich chocolate cake, served in slices with fresh cream.

Christmas cake   Soft cake with icing; tucked between the icing and cake is marzipan.

Christmas pudding   A plum cake or plum pudding served with a rich sauce. Often, there's a coin baked in it for luck.

cloak   A long coat that wraps around the body and fastens near the neck but may not have actual sleeves; like a thick poncho.

clotted cream   Thick cream made from scalded milk.

codswollop   Hogwash; baloney. *See also* tripe.

collywobbles   The willies.

copper   Police officer.

cracker A British holiday traditional favor that's roughly the size of a paper towel tube, or smaller. When you pull the cracker apart, it makes a loud "bang!" and out come small treats or even small, inexpensive gifts.

crikey Golly.

crumpet Unsweetened cake that's cooked like a pancake, but is taller and not as large in diameter as pancakes are.

cupboard Closet.

cuppa Cup of tea.

custard Sweet mix of milk and eggs that's usually baked but may also be boiled.

dab hand Good at; excellent.

derby *See* bowler hat.

dodgy Scary; risky; rundown; unreliable; dirty.

done a runner Run away; escaped.

dozy Stupid.

draught British spelling of "draft."

dustbin Trash can.

football British term for soccer.

fortnight Two weeks.

four-poster Bed.

fussed Bothered.

garden Backyard.

git Jerk.

gob Spit.

gobstruck Astonished.

going spare Going crazy.

gone round the twist Gone crazy.

have a go at Make fun of or lay into.

haversack A small backpack or any sort of bag carried on one's back or shoulder by a strap.

head *See* headmaster; headmistress.

Head Boy *See* prefect.

Head Girl *See* prefect.

headmaster The man in charge of a boarding school.

headmistress The woman in charge of a boarding school.

hotel Place to stay the night that generally will *not* have a bar on the premises, although it will usually serve breakfast. Also called a private hotel.

house A grouping of boarding-school students; students live together and compete for best house in intra-school competitions.

inn Place to stay the night that may or may not have a bar that serves alcoholic beverages, but it always offers meals.

jot Bit; iota.

keen Eager.

King's Cross Train station in London.

kip A nap.

kippers Salt-cured (often smoked) dried fish; usually made from herring.

knickerbocker glory Ice cream dessert.

knickerbockers Dressy short pants like those golfers used to wear.

lift Elevator.

lintel The upper portion of a doorway frame or window frame.

looking daggers Giving evil looks.

marmalade   *See* toast and marmalade.

mate   Pal; buddy; dude.

mead   A sweet wine made from honey and sometimes aged in oak barrels.

mental   Crazy.

meringue   A dessert with a meringue crust (like a pie crust but made of meringue) topped with fruit or other sweet fillings.

mince   Another word for ground beef or other meat chopped up into tiny bits.

mince pie   Sweet pie made of mincemeat that's either served cold with custard or clotted cream or heated with brandy butter.

mincemeat   Sweet pie filling, usually consisting of apples, raisins, beef fat, and (sometimes) mince.

mind the gap   Watch your step as you cross from the edge of a carriage (train car) and the platform.

moleskin   Originally, the fur of a mole, used for outerwear. Now also used to denote a heavy cotton fabric.

mollycoddling   Treating like a child.

mouth organ   Harmonica.

nick   Steal.

nip   Going somewhere quickly and/or briefly.

nutter   Crazy person.

Paddington Station   Train station in London.

pastilles   Fruit candies coated in sugar that come twelve to a pack.

pasty   A flaky crust that fully surrounds a rather dry filling of beef or chicken, potatoes, onions, and other ingredients. Also called a Cornish pasty.

pence   Plural of penny, which is one one-hundredth of a British pound.

peppermint humbugs   Hard candy flavored with peppermint oil.

pitch   An area of land used as a grassy playing field.

plait   Pleat (such as the pleat of a skirt).

platform   The area at which passengers board a train.

porkpie   Small pastry with a SPAM-like pork product in the middle; often served with gravy.

porridge   Crushed oats or oatmeal (and, occasionally, other grains) boiled in water and/or milk and usually served with sugar and cream.

prat   An uptight, goody-two-shoes airbrain.

prefect   The top boy or girl at a school. Also called Head Boy or Head Girl.

pub   A bar or bar/inn combination.

public school   British boarding school.

pudding   Another word for dessert.

queue   A line of people, such as one at a bus stop, stadium entrance, or lunch line.

ruddy   Darned.

sacked   Fired.

scrum   Rugby term that in non-Rugby settings usually means skirmish.

Sellotape   A brand of tape (like the American Scotch tape).

shut your gob   Shut up.

skive   Skip school.

Snap   Children's card game, played with two or more players.

spiffing   To make wonderful, great.

spotted dick   A confection made with suet (beef fat), rubbed into flour and made into a pudding, and then given some dried fruit; served with custard.

taking the mickey   To tease or ridicule.

tart   An individual pie; a crust is topped with fresh fruit, jam, cream, and/or custard.

television aerial   TV antennae.

toast and marmalade   Toast and jam; the marmalade is usually made with oranges.

treacle fudge   Fudge made with treacle.

treacle pudding   A steamed pudding made with treacle.

treacle tart   A tart topped with treacle.

treacle   A syrupy topping, with a consistency something like corn syrup but usually made with molasses.

trifle   A many-layered confection that begins with sponge cake (sometimes soaked in rum or other liqueur), then fruit, then cream, and so on.

tripe   Stomach of a cow or ox; eaten as a delicacy. Also called codswollop.

trolley   Food cart that travels down the aisles of a train car.

Turkish Delight   A candy that's a denser, chewier version of marshmallow, coated in sugar, with either chocolate or sprinkles on top.

wardrobe   A large cabinet that acts as a closet.

wastrel   A lazy person.

West Ham United Football Club   Soccer club located in east London.

wotcher   Hello!; what's up?

wrench   A difficult decision.

Yorkshire pudding   A hearty side dish similar to an American popover. May be served with horseradish sauce and/or gravy.

Appendix B

Cool Wizarding Websites

With hundreds (and even thousands) of new Harry Potter Internet sites appearing each month, you may want to know where to turn first. Here are my picks for the most interesting, up-to-date, and easy-to-navigate sites.

The Top Sites

We start with the best of the best.

J.K. Rowling's Site (www.jkrowling.com)

If you're going to get information, go straight to the source. Launched in 2004, this site is full of fun details about Rowling's life, work, writing process, and news. There's a cool list of links, too. While books were in process, the site was updated regularly; whether that will continue after the release of the final novel in the series remains to be seen.

Harry Potter Lexicon (www.hp-lexicon.org)

The Harry Potter Lexicon is an encyclopedia of Harry Potter facts. Information is arranged logically and is easily searchable. So when you're arguing with your friends about whether Hermione's middle name is Anastasia or Jane, check it out here. (It's Jane.)

Fan Sites

There are thousands of Harry Potter fan sites, and each offers something slightly different. If the ones listed here don't work for you, search around, find one you like, bookmark it, and check it every week! In addition to the sites discussed in the following sections, a few others you may want to check out are www.hpana.com (for good, quick updates), www.darkmark.com, and www.veritaserum.com.

The Leaky Cauldron (www.the-leaky-cauldron.org)

Run by fans, The Leaky Cauldron is news-central for anything and everything related to *Harry Potter.* Movie trailers are posted almost the moment they come out, as are any interviews with J.K. Rowling and actors from the movies.

PotterCast (www.pottercast.com)

Officially part of The Leaky Cauldron site, Pottercast is a weekly hour-long podcast of interesting and unique news, interviews, and fan commentary you won't hear in the mainstream media.

Harry Potter Fan Zone (www.harrypotterfanzone.com)

The Harry Potter Fan Zone (HPFZ) was started by an Australian teenager and has grown to require the efforts of almost two dozen people. As Harry Potter news happens, this site reports it.

Muggle Net (www.mugglenet.com)

News, fan commentary, competitions, and discounted shopping make this fan site unique. Check out the always-interesting Wall of Shame, which is a posting of some disturbing correspondence the webmaster has received. Also check out MuggleCast (www.mugglecast.com), which features weekly podcasts in which theories and rumors are discussed and debated.

Movie and Actor Sites

The movies based on Rowling's novels are nearly as big of a phenomenon as the novels themselves. Here are sites that are devoted to the Harry Potter movies or to the actors who play significant roles.

Warner Brothers (http://harrypotter.warnerbros.com)

This is the official Warner Brothers site, so it offers brilliantly vivid movie clips and trailers. It is not updated regularly, however. You can also visit http://harrypotter.warnerbros.co.uk for the British viewpoint, although the sites are roughly the same.

Daniel Radcliffe (www.danradcliffe.com)

Devoted to the actor who plays Harry Potter in the movies, this site is part movie promotion, part public relations, and part charity fundraising. But it all comes together in a nice package, including interviews, articles, and a calendar of appearances.

Travel-Related Sites

If you're planning to travel and want to visit Harry Potter–related sites, check out the Tourist Tip sidebars throughout this book. And also check out HP Fan Trips (www.hpfantrips.com), which arranges trips based on the novels and movies. If you have the time and cash, you definitely want to take the Hogwarts Express train ride! You can also search for other Harry Potter travel sites by using an Internet search engine.

Merchandise Sites

Want your own holly wand with a unicorn's tail as the core? Need a great wizarding hat for your next party? Want to get your hands on Bertie Bott's Every-Flavor Beans? These sites help you spend your hard-earned cash on wizard products of all types.

Alivans (www.alivans.com)

Modeled to look and feel like Ollivanders (see Chapter 7), this site is among the best Harry Potter merchandise sites on the web. The website is set up like the interactive DVD tours that come with the first two Harry Potter movies. The illusion is so complete that you actually feel like a wizard ordering a wand, broom, clothing, etc. (Of course, there's no Internet in the wizarding world, but that's a small point.) If you're considering a wand for yourself or to give as a gift, this is where to buy it. You'll pay more than at other sites, but your wand will be made of the finest wood with excellent craftsmanship. The brooms, too, are incredibly authentic.

The Official Warner Brothers Shop (http://harrypotter.wbshop.com)

From T-shirts and hats to action figures and a collectible Time Turner, this slick site is the official site of movie-related Harry Potter products. Be sure to order your Harry Potter tree ornaments well in advance of the holidays!

Harry Gear (www.harrygear.com)

Billed as carrying "official" Harry Potter products, Harry Gear offers high quality hats, scarves—even glasses and Quidditch goggles! The online store doesn't carry many products, but the ones it carries look and feel authentic. Shipping is a flat $5.95 fee per order.

The Order of Merlin (www.orderofmerlin.com)

This rather kitschy online store is devoted to all things Harry Potter. Even if items are relatively useless (as is likely the case with a cast-iron cauldron, the laminated Apparator's License, and the ten-pack of parchment paper), The Order of Merlin offers gobs of Harry Potter gifts at reasonable prices.

Whimsicalley (www.whimsicalley.com)

Set up like a mall of authentic wizard stores you can link to, at Whimsicalley, you can stock up on Harry Potter products to your heart's content, from wands to robes to books. You can even purchase a bottle of Felix Felicis. Prices are usually quite reasonable.

The Feelings Company (www.feelingscompany.com)

This store specializes in hats, not Harry Potter memorabilia, but its
wizard hats are so authentic-looking and reasonably priced that this site
is worth a mention. Click on Fantasy Hats and Helmets when you get to
the home page.

LEGO (www.lego.com/eng/harrypotter)

Oh my gosh! If you like LEGO toys, there just isn't anything cuter
than the Harry Potter–themed LEGO sets. Products range from Harry
Potter keychains to the Hogwarts Express train set to entire kits and
games that reenact scenes from the novels. Like all LEGO products,
prices tend to be on the steep side, but they also last a lifetime. Another
downside is that products appear to be limited edition, so some sell out
and are no longer available—at least not in the United States.

eBay (www.ebay.com)

Before you spend full price on anything, first check out eBay and view
current auctions for everything related to Harry Potter. But *caveat emptor:*
if a seller claims to have an item "autographed by J.K. Rowling," assume
it's a fake.

Sylvan Lane Shoppe (www.sylvanlaneshoppe.com/ WBharry_potter.htm)

Much of what's available at Honeydukes (see Chapter 8) is available at
Sylvan Lane Shoppe—Fizzing Whizbees, Cockroach Clusters, Acid
Pops, Jelly Slugs, Bertie Bott's Every Flavor Beans, Chocolate Frogs, and
more! Although the company experiences distribution problems from
time to time, when they get stock in, it's the real deal. You can buy small
quantities, too, because not everyone needs a dozen packs of Ice Mice.

Candy Warehouse (www.candywarehouse.com/harrypotter. html)

Candy Warehouse offers a similar selection to that of Sylvan Lane, but
candies are rarely out of stock. Plus, while you're there, you can also get
Willy Wonka candy, *Star Wars* candy, and Disney candy. The downside
is that nearly all candy needs to be ordered in bulk.

British Delights (www.britishdelights.com)

An online opportunity to purchase much of the British food discussed in Chapter 4, British Delights (operated out of Westford, Massachusetts) offers everything from bangers to mince pie to Yorkshire pudding, all with reasonable shipping times and fees.

Fan Fiction Sites

Fan fiction refers to a site full of stories written by fans (not by Rowling) that use the Harry Potter characters and settings in fresh ways. Fan fiction is written by children and adults alike, and some of it is sugar-sweet, some borders on erotic, and most of it lies somewhere in between. The biggest is Fiction Alley (www.fictionalley.org). Harry Potter Fan Fiction (www.harrypotterfanfiction.com) is another of the most prolific of the fan fiction sites; if you don't like what you find at either of those, search on "Harry Potter fan fiction" for an overload of similar sites. Parents should keep in mind that some fan fiction is not suitable for children. Fan fiction is usually rated by the authors using a system similar to movie ratings (G to NC-17).

Index